BEHIND THE SCREENS

PROGRAMMERS REVEAL HOW FILM FESTIVALS REALLY WORK

Originally published by ReelPlan Press, August, 2012

Revised version published by ReelPlan Press, November, 2015

Author photo by Tom Kochel, kochel.com

Printed in the United States of America

ReelPlan Consulting
916 G Street NW. Studio 203
Washington, DC 20001
reelplan.com

ISBN-13: 978-1477692516
ISBN-10: 1477692517
LCCN: 2012913542

ACKNOWLEDGMENTS

I could not have undertaken this project without the support of my friends and colleagues who guided me through.

First, a special thanks to my mother, Judy Gann, and interns Daniel Shor, Emma Wimmer and Shilah Alibakhsi for painstakingly transcribing the audio interviews and researching the subjects. For the updated version, a heartfelt thanks to John Bickley for researching and adding links to the web and Kindle versions.

My long-time producer, Sohini Baliga, was instrumental in editing, proofreading and standardizing the material into a unified collection. Thank you.

Everyone should befriend a poet. Not only did the fabulous Kim Roberts edit the interviews, she organized weekly hikes to escape office pressures and provide a much-needed sound board.

For the past few years, my mentor and friend, Kelley Baker, goaded me to call on my friends and ask them about what makes them tick. At first, I resisted, but am now glad that I have created this important resource. I will always be grateful.

This book was made possible through a grant by the D.C. Commission on the Arts and Humanities. *dcarts.dc.gov*

TABLE OF CONTENTS

INTRODUCTION

"Is your film going to be at Sundance?'

I can't tell you how many times I've heard that question from both filmmakers and non-filmmakers. It's as if there is only one film festival in the whole world and naturally they're going to show our films.

Do you have any idea how many films get submitted to Sundance every year? 8,500. Know how many are actually screened? 83!

And doesn't include the films that have been invited to screen and don't have to go through the regular submission process.

Are you aware that there are other film festivals besides *Sundance?* A whole bunch of them. And Sundance is not the only film festival that matters! Just because you don't get in your career is not over. Depending on the kind of film you've made, there might be better film festivals for your work.

You've spent two years (or more) making your film and now you need to get it out so people can see it. That's where film festivals can help. If you're a filmmaker, you need to do your homework and figure out what film festival is best for you.

What is your film about? Who is your audience?

I know, you think your film deals with universal themes and your film is for everyone. But there's no such thing as a general audience. Your film is not for everyone and not all film festivals are chomping at the bit to get it.

As Jon Gann says, "There is a festival for every film, but not every film is right for every festival." And he's right. Jon takes you behind the scenes and talks with film festival directors who give us insight as to what motivates their decision-making process.

When Jon told me he was writing this book I knew he was the perfect person to do it. In addition to founding and running his own film festival, DC Shorts, Jon is also a filmmaker so he truly understands the filmmaker's point of view.

A little background here. I am a touring filmmaker, so every year I spend four-to-six months on the road showing my films, guest lecturing, and participating on panels at film festivals, universities, media art centers, and just about any place else they'll let me in.

For years Jon has been saying that he wanted to go out on tour with me, so in the fall of 2010 Jon and his dog, Pilot, accompanied me for the final month of my tour. I taught "Self-Distribution and Marketing" and Jon taught "Film Festival Strategies." It was an eye opener!

I have been going to the DC Shorts Film Festival and teaching workshops there for years. It's one of the high points of my year. I thought I knew a lot about festivals as I have been entering and attending them since the mid 1980s. (I still remember when you had to submit your films in either 16mm or 35mm. Now we upload our films to secure sites on the Internet and they play off computers in the theaters.)

I've been to festivals and seen filmmakers treated like shit. I've seen filmmakers treat audiences and festival staff like shit. I've been treated like shit at some festivals. And I'll admit to writing and saying a lot of things about festivals that weren't exactly complimentary.

After touring with Jon, I found out just how much work goes in to putting a festival together. I also found out just how many filmmakers are submitting films to festivals these days, and how many of these are truly bad films.

More often than not, filmmakers aren't reading the guidelines and instructions and they're sending their films to the wrong festivals. (Please don't send your romantic comedy to the Chicago Underground Film Festival; it probably won't get in.) And festival entry fees aren't cheap!

Jon shows us how film festivals really work, and we get to meet some of the people who run them. And you know what? Most festivals are run by people who truly love movies. They feel it's their mission to expose audiences to new and different work. And they put up with a lot to do it. They have to raise money, find sponsors, book venues, arrange publicity, call for entries, watch hundreds of movies, organize films in themes that make sense, schedule the festival and all of the surrounding events, and after all that, they have to deal with us, the filmmakers.

Why so many of these people continue to do it year after year is beyond me. They put up with our stupid questions and our complaints. (And why is it that the filmmakers who complain the most about their films not getting in are usually the filmmakers with the worst films? Just sayin'…)

Jon pulls back the curtain so we can see what these film festival directors think about and how they make decisions. Is it important to have a big star in your movie? Or is it more important to have a good, well-told story? Do sponsors pressure festivals to show certain films?

As filmmakers we get pissed. We think, "Why should I have to pay to get into a festival? I paid for my movie! They should be paying me! Who are these people? What do they want? What can a film festival do for me anyway? How come they didn't take my movie? I know it's better than the crap they're showing." And on and on…

In this book you'll get answers to all these questions and more.

You'll also find out how to alienate festival directors (drink too much and be obnoxious at the parties, or complain about the projection to everyone within ear shot), things to do so that your film won't ever be selected (uncleared music and really bad sound), and please, don't ask these folks to waive the fee for their festival — you should have budgeted for that.

These film festival directors are extremely open about what they're looking for and why they actually want to help filmmakers reach an audience. This book is so full of good, practical advice that even an old film festival veteran like me learned a lot.

Jon also tells you what you need to do to have a good and successful experience at a festival. Short answer: Promote your screening once you get there, take lots of DVDs, hand out postcards. Also, make yourself accessible to the audience and it will pay dividends.

Read, learn, and enjoy. Then figure out what your film is about, who your audience is, and send it to the right festival. The odds are better that you'll get in.

And if not, don't come crawling to me. I tried to steer you in the right direction.

Now leave me alone, I've got work to do...

Kelley Baker
The Angry Filmmaker

"WHY DID MY FILM NOT GET IN?"

"Everyone thinks my film is great! You guys don't know what is really good."

"I've seen the films you program and mine is so much better."

"My film won awards at four other festivals! I don't understand why you didn't pick it up."

I receive these complaints (and worse) daily from filmmakers of every level of experience — from novice high school students to award-winning directors. I'm going to probably surprise you and say your film wasn't rejected because it sucked — although that can definitely be a factor. The real reasons are complex and varied, but come down to a single factor: *film festivals are not necessarily what you think.*

Film festivals are a business to showcase outstanding films to established audiences, attract new audiences, and provide a solid platform for filmmakers to meet and connect with these audiences and one another. That's a lot of planets to align, and sometimes the math just may not work in your favor. It really is that simple.

But everyone can agree on this basic premise: The desires of filmmakers and the needs of festival programmers are often at odds. And these often-competing interests mean that it's your job, as a filmmaker, to create an informed festival strategy for your film with care.

The programmers in this collection of interviews have the same concerns: primarily that most filmmakers do not have an appropriate (or any) festival strategy. Tired after the arduous process of writing, funding, shooting and editing their masterpiece, many filmmakers simply choose festivals from a list of big-name events or submit their project based on media buzz and fancy web sites, but they don't research to learn if the event is a proper fit for their film. Millions of dollars are wasted every year on pipe dreams and vanity career moves. With a few days of internet research, well-crafted emails and strategic phone calls, filmmakers could enter 50 festivals with a 10% return (on average) or enter 10 appropriate events with a 90% return. Think of the money saved on entry fees, disc duplication, press kits and shipping — and the frustration of rejection letters.

Festival programmers are under a great deal of pressure to please sponsors, distributors, funders, and boards. They must deal with scheduling concerns, venue availability, subject matter and taste issues, and the glut of similarly themed films that naturally occur every year.

But their greatest pressure is to appeal to audiences — every festival has a unique personality. One might be "crunchy and green" even though they screen bigger studio films. Another might be "preppy and conservative" although their late-night lineup might make a hooker blush. Their taste for dramas, comedies, documentary, experimental — short or long format — subtitled or silent — all vary from city to city. More frustrating is that even within the same events, audiences can vary greatly depending on time of day, location of the theater, the weather, or events happening in the news.

These personalities start with the programmers. While feelings are usually checked at the door, we're human and we all love films for very personal reasons. On top of these influences are often factors you might never have considered, including workplace stresses, the frustration of random technical gremlins, and "film numbness" from watching and reviewing hundreds (sometimes thousands) of submissions. Ultimately, our final selections create the mood and zeitgeist of the event — which we hope entices, satisfies and builds a paying audience.

I have been fortunate enough to see the world of festivals from both sides (you can read more of my story in the last chapter.) As a filmmaker, I've traveled the globe to support films I wrote and directed. As a guest, I've enjoyed the hospitality offered by festival organizers, meeting audiences along the way. As a festival director, I have been fortunate enough to meet hundreds of other festival organizers, and have spent a great deal of time talking to them, asking questions about their systems and processes, and working to network for an open exchange of information — an open exchange I now bring to you.

So how should you read this book? Look for the consistencies between the interviews — there are many. Then look at what makes each festival different. It's these differences that ultimately allow each festival to reach its audience. But most importantly, read between the lines. While I am very grateful that these programmers have been so open and honest, providing a unique and privileged insight into their minds, even in their honesty, there are veiled facts which you need to discover — and consider. The festival facts at the beginning of each interview provide an insight as to what each event has to work with: the number of submissions, the demographics of their audience, their organization's mission — and their (often shockingly small) budgets from which they must plan, program, promote and produce their festivals.

If one filmmaker reads this book and learns why it is critical to read the submission rules, or package a DVD so it doesn't shatter in shipping, or remembers to keep their cool at a screening in the midst of a projection catastrophe, then this "behind the screens" look into the realities of the festival world will have the desired effect — to level the playing field and create an atmosphere where filmmakers can create even better content that festivals will want to program — and audiences will love.

"EVALUATE. CURATE. CONNECT." LAURA HENNEMAN

Former Senior Programmer, Napa Valley Film Festival
Former Programming Committee, Ashland Independent Film Festival

About the Festival:

- Founded in 2011, the Napa Valley Film Festival showcases the best in new independent filmmaking and world cinema.
- 5-day event for general audiences
- Website: napavalleyfilmfest.org

A native of the Pacific Northwest, Laura Henneman has been a film festival professional for over eight years. Shortly after earning her film degree from Boston University, Laura began volunteering at the Ashland Independent Film Festival (AIFF). She was quickly hired as the Filmmaker Liaison and spent six seasons with AIFF, helping to grow the Festival into a highly respected regional event known among filmmaking communities for treating independent filmmakers like rock stars.

Between AIFF seasons, Laura was free to be a film festival gypsy and worked to bring films, filmmakers and audiences together in formats ranging from touring festivals, to animation-only events, to international start-ups. She was a founding staff member and film programmer with both the Middle East International Film Festival (then the Abu Dhabi Film Festival, now the SANAD Abu Dhabi Film Fund)) and the Napa Valley Film Festival and was invited to rejoin AIFF as a programmer in the 2012 season.

JON: Napa Valley is one of the newest festivals on the circuit. How did it begin, and how did you get involved?

LAURA: Brenda and Marc Lhormer founded the Festival after producing and distributing their first feature film *Bottle Shock*, which premiered at Sundance in 2008. Previously, the Lhormers ran the Sonoma Valley Film Festival for seven years, building it up from a struggling local event to a highly regarded regional destination festival.

I had met the Lhormers at various festivals and summits over the years. In December 2010 I reconnected with them at IFFS (the International Film Festival Summit). They were staffing up for NVFF and I had just wrapped up another festival contract and was looking for a long-term programming position. The stars were aligned!

What's your film or festival background?

I attended film school at Boston University for screenwriting and film production but by the time I graduated I wasn't sure film*making* was the right path for me. After graduating I came home to Ashland, Oregon and started volunteering for the Ashland Independent Film Festival (AIFF). Shortly after that the filmmaker liaison position opened up and I was offered the job! That was my anchor festival for six years and I did freelance work for other festivals during AIFF's "off-season." So I sort of just fell into this world, but it's a good fit and I've been lucky enough to make a career in it.

Have you had a lot of film-related jobs?

Outside of festivals, not many since film school. I've done a little on-set production and script supervising, but programming and festival work has really been my focus.

I know that you have been somewhat of a "Festival Gypsy." Can you explain?

For many years I worked a rotating series of seasonal (i.e. short term) positions at different festivals and that's how I was able to both stay in the festival world and build my experience. Most festivals have some year-round staff, and many festival professionals can stay in one place. But nearly all staffs expand seasonally, and that's where the gypsies come in.

I've also chosen to be a festival gypsy so I can work in the specific areas of festivals that interest me: film programming and filmmaker relations. In my experience, long-term position openings in those departments are few and far between, so I've followed the work where it takes me. My current programming work with AIFF and NVFF has allowed me to stay in one, well, two places for some time and that has been great.

Moving from community to community can be fantastic, and it can be trying.

There's not a lot of money in this field, so working in different places has been the way I can afford to "travel." Through this work I've seen a lot more of the country and the world than I would have otherwise!

Before you got involved with Napa, did you attend other festivals?

I did, but infrequently, mainly because to sustain myself as a festival gypsy I was working at least two, and up to four, festivals a year, leaving little time to attend others. Believe it or not, the first festival I really attended (with a credential, seeing three and four films a day) was Cannes when I was in college. I was studying abroad in Paris and working for the Cinémathèque Française. Lucky for me they invited the American intern to come along to the Festival — what an incredible experience!

Now, as a programmer, how many festivals do you attend in a year?

In 2011 I really only got to AIFF because it was the first year for Napa and I was completely consumed with getting NVFF up and running. My experience of festivals last year was all through their websites and program books! For 2012 I'll probably manage to get to about three or four, and I'd like to see that increase as we settle down a bit. But, you know, as a founding staff member, you're kind of tied to your desk.

Which festivals do you admire? What parts would you like to take away and implement at NVFF?

I went to SXSW [South by Southwest] for the first time this year and was very impressed by their operational organization. It's a massive event but the way they run venues and publicize screening information makes it manageable.

I've always enjoyed the Seattle International Film Festival. They have such a wide range of programming, great community engagement, and a sense of fun and festival about the whole event.

Obviously I'm partial, but I really think the AIFF has a lot going for it. Their community support is so strong, it's a really open-minded audience. Practically every screening sells out and their audience is phenomenally engaged. And even if it's a situation where people don't entirely *love* the film, they can *appreciate* the film, which isn't necessarily the case for a lot of audiences.

I agree with you. Attending Ashland was one of the motivations for me to create DC Shorts. Can you describe the submission and selection process at NVFF?

We are listed on Withoutabox, so the submission process is pretty standard. When a film arrives in the office it gets cataloged and circulated with our group of volunteer community screeners who watch it and write reviews. I go through all the reviews, and the films that were highly rated filter up to the programming group. We screen the films, write our own programming notes, and put the titles of the top films on sticky notes on my office wall — the last step in the review process and the first step towards selection and scheduling. Those notes get moved around into screening tracks and scheduling slots, it's a way to visualize the list of potential films. Sticky notes are very big in this process!

How many people are on the initial committee?

The community screening group is made up of around a dozen people. We try to have at least two people see each submission all the way through, and then we take their reviews from there. Sometimes more people see a film if the initial reviews are mixed, and if the film gets really polarized scores I usually take a look at it myself.

What percentage of the committee are film professionals?

At this point in Napa, very few. We have some screeners who have some experience in film, but really the intent is for the committee to be a broad sample of the community. What does the local community want to see, what are they interested in?

What qualities do you think make for a good community screener?

First of all, a passionate, deep, and broad interest in film. Beyond that, it's very much about the ability to communicate your ideas. Being able to explain, not just, "Yes, I liked it," or, "No, I didn't like it," but why — and then articulate specifics. The programmers want to look at a review in terms of, "these are this film's red flags, and these are its strengths." Being able to write about film and communicate your opinions are key qualities.

Who is on the selection committee?

The selection committee is primarily myself, and Executive & Artistic Director Marc Lhormer, who is one of the festival founders, with co-founder Brenda Lhormer.

Is the process the same if you "curate in" a film?

When we invite someone to send us their film for review, it typically goes straight to the programming team. If it's caught our interest, there's a reason for it and we don't generally have to ask our screeners to spend time generating an initial set of reviews. After the programmers watch the film it may be sent to the screening committee if we feel we need more opinions.

How long is your submission period?

We open the call for entries at the end of January and close in June. We're watching films and crafting the line-up through the summer and announce the program in October, both online and with the printed program book. It's an extended process because we get our book out well in advance of the event. Last year was Napa's first festival, so it was important to get that material out into the hands of the audience and press so they knew what the Festival was about and had time to plan their attendance and coverage.

Do you charge a submission fee? What is the justification?

We do charge submission fees. We're a non-profit festival and fees cover the cost of running the submission process. I think it's important for filmmakers to know it doesn't serve anyone if a filmmaker just blankets the festival world with their film. So submission fees, while an indirect way to do it, is one tool to get submitters to look at a festival more thoroughly and decide: "Is this the right place for my film, do I have a good chance of meeting the criteria, and is my film a good match for the festival audience?" Money is a motivating factor and a submission fee helps to minimize those blanket submissions.

And the fees are used for?

The fees essentially pay for submission processing and tracking, and to support the programming process. It takes staff time to catalog and keep track of entries, to coordinate the screening committee, to publicize the call for entries, to communicate with filmmakers about their submissions. We're definitely not looking to make income from of it — it's more of an offset for the process.

I don't think a lot of filmmakers understand that systems like Withoutabox are expensive. They have heavy fees and take a large percentage of the submission fee for the convenience of using their software.

Right. And to handle the volume of submissions it takes to craft a quality film line-up you need that type of a collection system. I don't think many festivals treat submissions as a revenue source. You're really looking to break even, to pay for the system itself and staff time.

Do you take online screeners? What are your thoughts on them?

We do, and I'm torn. It's something I've struggled with in the last couple of years, because I love the convenience of online screeners, but it does present a challenge with the logistical side of tracking films and feeling like you have a centralized pool of entries. Now we must track DVDs, online screeners through Withoutabox, and requested screeners on other systems like Vimeo or other online sites. It has necessitated a bit of a shift in terms of how we structure our process of making sure every film is viewed, tracking which screener has which materials, where films can be accessed, etc. On a practical note, I don't love the functionality of the Withoutabox online viewer. And once a film is selected, we ultimately need a DVD copy anyway. So online screeners might save a step for some films, but create steps for others.

As a matter of course, do you give feedback to filmmakers, or is it something you do when people ask?

Regretfully, we're only able to give feedback when people ask. I wish that weren't the case, but at this point it's just a bandwidth issue — hundreds of films, a small group of programmers.

When you're making decisions, do you find media kits helpful at all? Do you even ask for them?

We do request media kits, but I try to judge an entry on the merit of the film alone. After all, the audience isn't going to see the media kit — they're just going to see the film. That said, if a film comes in with a really polished, well-produced media kit, I can't help the fact that it may make me think, "Hmm, this film is possibly more promising." I'm human.

The reason we ask for a media kit up front is that if film does get in, we're that much closer to having the materials we need to publicize it and put our program book and festival website together. A great alternative to sending a press kit with the submission is having a comprehensive EPK [electronic press kit] and website, so the materials are all there for the festival to access. The media kit in whatever form is more about streamlining the future, rather than affecting the submission and programming period.

What's the biggest mistake a filmmaker can make when submitting to a film festival?

Not reading the entry criteria or following the entry guidelines: it's as simple as that. So many films come in incorrectly categorized, or without a running time listed. Also, it sounds really, really, simple and basic and inane, but labeling your materials makes a huge difference — we need to know the title, entry number, running time, contact number, and name of the submitter. If something goes wrong — a DVD doesn't play, whatever — and we have all that information on your disc, it's so much easier to work with you to bring the film to the festival.

Do you pay screening fees?

Screening fees generally come up only with films we've requested, not standard submissions. We managed to avoid paying screening fees in the first year of NVFF. In place of fees, we usually propose the alternative of travel and hospitality for the filmmaker — which I think is a bigger benefit for everyone, because our audience gets to meet the filmmaker, and the filmmaker gets to enjoy the Festival.

Does NVFF have a prize system?

NVFF has both jury and audience awards. We're lucky enough to have a sponsor who has supported our U.S. narrative feature award to the tune of $10,000. Getting to hand that prize to the winning filmmaker is amazing and speaks to both what we're trying to do as a festival and my personal goal as a programmer: to support independent film and filmmakers! We're trying to create prize packages for the feature documentary and shorts categories also.

For accepted filmmakers, do you offer travel, lodging, and food?

We offer lodging to everyone; travel on a case-by-case basis. It depends on what our travel partners have given us. Last year, we had an airline partner provide a limited number of flight vouchers for filmmakers. But hospitality is definitely a cornerstone of our mission, so we try to provide housing for all filmmakers who can attend.

What elements do you think add up to make a successful film? What are the elements you are looking for that say, "this film works for me"?

For me, it's all about storytelling. It starts with an interesting story, with compelling characters. Production value is also important, but if a film's story is strong and the look isn't as polished I would still consider it. After all, the look of a narrative could be an artistic choice, or a documentary might have been made under circumstances that didn't allow for the production standards you might otherwise expect.

I'm also looking for a film that uses the medium well. Why is this a film, as opposed to a radio piece, an essay, a painting, something else? I have seen a lot of documentaries where they're exploring an interesting topic, but the filmmakers didn't use the medium of film to their advantage in any way; it's just sort of a video essay. I don't want to call that a film, I want to call it something else.

I think you just did; it's a video essay. I think the problem, especially with a documentary, is so many people feel that the only way to express their point is through the creation of a documentary film, as opposed to a nice NPR-style radio piece, or a well-crafted essay or editorial piece. Maybe that's because the distribution opportunities for a documentary are so much greater than the distribution of a radio program.

Is it though? If you got on *This American Life* more people are going to hear it than if a documentary screens at a couple of film festivals.

I would agree, but I think the competition to get into This American Life *would be more difficult than to play a bunch of festivals. And let's face it — film is sexy and radio is not. So everyone wants to get into the thing that's sexy.*

Good point. A shorthand term for that type of a "film" would be useful to explain if a piece is something worth showing because of the value of its subject, even though it is not a "film" in the traditional, more artistic sense. If the subject is compelling enough, there's a place for these video essays as well.

However, when I'm knee-deep in programming I do encounter pieces that make me think, "Does this need to be a film?" So one thing that filmmakers should consider when planning a film is how to use the medium to their best advantage.

What are some of your red flags — the things that make you want to click off the DVD player?

Films that use excessive slow motion, soft focus shots of children playing to express a sense of innocence and purity. I just saw yet another film with this cliché yesterday so that's top of mind. And butterfly imagery is really over used, too.

Seriously though, bad sound quality drives me crazy. Thankfully, that seems to be less of a problem than it was even just a few years ago; maybe it's simply technology improving. But if a filmmaker didn't mic the actors or interview subjects correctly, if they simply used a camera's onboard microphone so the room tone is overwhelming, or if they didn't address sound in post production, that's a big problem and often indicates there will be other issues with the film. Sound quality is probably my biggest immediate red flag.

Other pet peeves include credits that are practically longer than a short film.

I agree with you on that one.

And although this is a little nit picky, I dislike the approach of using the Hollywood structure of opening titles for an independent film. I really just want you to get to the story and tell me about the cast and crew at the end, once I've seen their work.

Do you have any taboos? Are there any subject matters you just can't program?

Personally, no, I don't think so. At least I've yet to run into a film that was too far beyond the pale. I think it is more a question of a festival's audience — does the audience have taboos or are certain subjects off limits? I was recently on a programmer's panel where the question was asked, "What do you do with that film that has some shortcomings, but the filmmaker shows promise and you know their next project is going to be great? Or along the same lines, what do you do with a film that isn't quite right for your audience, or pushes your audience just a little too much, but you want to support the film and filmmaker?"

I'm lucky enough that NVFF has The Lounge, a venue that was created specifically to showcase films that push boundaries — in either a darker or lighter way. We program the sillier comedies and the darker, "edgier" films there, so they reach a more tailored, adventuresome audience. It's as close as Napa gets to genre programming. We promote that venue by saying to our audience, "Be aware, this isn't what you're going to see in your average multiplex. But if you're open to that you're probably going to like every film in this venue."

That's a great way of handling it. And it's always tough, because sometimes you see a film and you're like, "Wow, I really can't take it because of its subject, but this person is talented," and you know they're going on to great things. It's great that you're fortunate enough to have a venue for that.

We're very fortunate, and the audience responded well to the films. The right people found The Lounge at the inaugural Festival and I think the right people will go back to it in future years. From a programming point of view that was very satisfying to see and I believe the filmmakers benefitted from screening in that space.

What are your thoughts about premiere status? Is it important to you?

I recognize that it's important for a festival's publicity efforts and overall credibility to be able to say, "yes, we have a premiere," but I think that publicity angle is often given a little too much weight. Premiere status isn't very important to me personally, but I see how it can be good for the festival and hopefully landing a premiere draws more attention to all the other festival films too.

Are you influenced by the accolades films receive at other festivals?

Yes, but only to the point of requesting a film so our programming team can review it. We definitely won't program a film solely based on where it's screened before, but if it's done well at other festivals it's more likely to be on my radar to evaluate with our audience in mind.

And what about big names?

In the programming process I don't give too much weight to "stars" in independent films, and it's frustrating when an otherwise mediocre film coasts through the circuit on a name, potentially taking a screening slot away from a quality film with an unknown cast. Again, there still has to be a good story there and I try to leave the star factor out of it when I'm watching a film for its artistic and creative value.

From the larger perspective of the festival business model though, there is some inherent value in showing a film with name talent, especially if they attend the festival. That brings more publicity and audience and can be good for everybody — it's similar to premieres, that extra attention can provide exposure for the film program as a whole.

But if a film was mediocre, it doesn't matter if DeNiro is in it or not — you probably still won't take it?

Well, ideally, no, we wouldn't take it. But there are so many factors that get weighed within a festival like NVFF when a film like that comes up. I would like to say empirically, across the board, we would not take it, but you never know.

Okay. How important is your audience in your final selection process?

Very. A good match of films and audience is an important measure of success for a festival. When you're designing your final film line-up you have to consider many elements and your audience influences subject matter, focus, overall tone of a program. You're always trying to keep your festival's identity in mind — and your audience is a big part of that, so you want to be sure that you're presenting a slate of films that compliment each other and will be well-received by viewers. So yes, audience is very important.

Do you think it's the most important factor?

In general, yes, it outweighs many other elements. If you're not serving your audience, who are you serving? And the filmmakers are a part of that "audience" in that sense - it doesn't do a film any good to be shown to an audience that doesn't get it. Sometimes I feel like filmmakers think I'm just giving them a line when I decline their film, explaining that it isn't a good fit for the festival. But that's so often the truth! That's not to say you shouldn't challenge your audience, within reason. But if you're not bringing the right films and filmmakers for your festival's audience, no one's really getting a lot out of it.

Have you ever programmed a film that you thought was fantastic, but the audience just did not get it?

I actually had one the first year of NVFF. It was a filmmaker's debut feature and one of those situations where I know that down the line this filmmaker is going to do great work, and while the film we showed had some flaws, it was definitely good enough for us to program. It's not a film where you're instantly going to love it and tell all of your friends to go see it, but instead it's one of those films that sticks with you and keeps you thinking. During the programming process, every time the film was mentioned in the office, we had a 20-minute discussion about it — and that means something. It's not a perfect film, but it's a film with a vision and I value that.

But the audience reaction was kind of "Eh?"

The film did not do well in audience voting. But I have to trust that the "I'm still thinking about this movie" effect happened to at least some of the people who saw it. I wish that there was some way to go back to the audience and ask, "Now what do you think about the film?" We'll see — hopefully we'll get to show that filmmaker's next project and people will be glad they saw the first one too. Like I said before, challenging your audience (to a point) can be a good thing. Or, in this case my instincts fell short of matching a film and an audience, but you have to take chances sometimes, right?

What role, if any, do sponsors and donors play in your selection process?

I'm a purist and I would like money to not be involved at all. We do take board member, advisory council, and community member suggestions on themes they would like to see and explore, but sponsor involvement doesn't specifically dictate what we show.

So, if a sponsor came to you and said, "I need you to show this film," you would just say "Mmm...no."

If it's a film that doesn't make the cut on its own merit? Personally, I would say, "Mmm...no." I am lucky enough to be in the position of being able to focus on art for art's sake, and I usually don't have to grapple with the money issues or outside influence. But in Napa, the other programmers are the founders and directors of the Festival, so they would be the ones who ultimately have to make that decision.

What role do distributors play in your process? Are you often influenced by what's available and what's not available?

Sometimes, yes. Because Napa is at the end of the festival season going into Oscar time, we do pursue films that have distribution and are likely to do well in the award season, and those aren't always available. There can be a lot of back-and-forth with distributors about what we want to show as a special sneak preview screening and what we can have based on release dates, etc. We definitely did that dance in our first year, and I don't anticipate that changing.

Do you often find you are pressured by distributors to take certain films in order to get other films?

We have seen some of that but because of our placement in the calendar we run into conflicts with release dates more than that type of pressure. Again, having only gone through the one season with NVFF, it's hard to project this festival's experience, but I have seen that pressure happen here and at other festivals.

When you ultimately put your schedule together, how do you group films? Do you do program thematically, by venue availability, or audience?

We're in a unique situation where we have venues in four different towns up and down the Napa Valley. One of the elements that we have to think about is travelling with our films to play for the different audiences. All of the competition films play in at least three of the four towns over the five days of the Festival. So for feature length films, the scheduling is not thematic so much as it is geographical.

As far as shorts programs, we do try to group films thematically. My very analog process involves film titles on sticky notes (see, I told you they're very important) on my office wall. Once we've narrowed the field down to films we would like to show I spend a lot of time staring at those titles, thinking about the films and trying to let the programs emerge. Then it's a matter of plotting the sequencing so that the flow of the program showcases the films in the best way. It's like arranging an art exhibit. Putting those short film blocks together is one of my favorite parts of the programming process.

So you're putting together a 120-minute block. Do you sometimes need to jettison some films that just don't fit into the schedule? Or might have to pick another film because it fits the time restraints or theme of that program better?

The former more than the latter, which sometimes results in a film that I love getting sidelined when it just doesn't fit the time available. I hate that. It is important for filmmakers to know though — a programming team may have really liked your film but couldn't accept it because, for example, it didn't fit in a program, or didn't match the festival's mission or audience. Keeping your short film *short* is also very important – the format is all about effective, economic storytelling. It's really hard to program a short that's over 20 minutes long (and truthfully, the strongest shorts tend to be well under that).

In terms of short film programs I really try to keep that initial group of titles on post-it notes big enough so that there are many options for program themes. Those films won't all get in because of the limited number of screening slots, but they all meet the level of quality that we want to showcase. Then it's about figuring out which films make sense as a program, play off of each other, and have something more to say as a group.

What do you think is more important — schooling, or storytelling?

Storytelling. All the education in the world can't teach you how to tell a good story. You need to have a passion for that story, and you need to have a unique voice and a vision in the way you communicate that story. I don't really think that can be taught, though it can be refined. Tools to execute a vision can be taught, so education is important, but formal schooling definitely is not a requirement to be a good filmmaker — and I can say that with confidence as a film school graduate!

We have seen a recent proliferation of film schools. Do you think that is affecting the quality of the films coming to the festival circuit?

I think its has resulted in quantity possibly more than quality. Beyond production techniques and skills, the one area where I think film schools can be really effective, and I wish more would take this approach, is in emphasizing producing skills — the financial, budgeting, and business side of film.

Maybe I would rephrase my answer of schooling vs. storytelling by I adding the caveat: "Yes, schooling is important if you're learning to be a producer."

For getting a film out into the world, if you can find an effective film school that teaches the business side of production and distribution, then schooling is very important. For the film itself, storytelling trumps all.

Agreed. I see plenty of stuff from people who have never been to film school that is amazing because they're incredible storytellers. I have also seen works from top film schools that have little story value.

And it's so hard to decline those technically beautiful films that have no story, but story is king!

What industry websites and publications do you regularly read?

IndieWire and *Variety* are my mainstays, and frequently the only ones I have time to get to. But more and more I'm also paying attention to the blogs of individual filmmakers and curators, which are often illuminating and a lot of fun.

Is NVFF Academy considered? Do you think that matters to filmmakers when they are applying?

We are not at this point (NVFF hasn't been around long enough yet), and I think it does attract filmmakers who are paying attention. I've worked for one Academy qualifying festival and from what I've seen that status primarily affects the volume of submissions that come in the door. So it can give those festivals access to more films and, potentially, more quality films, but it also means more competition for the filmmakers who are applying.

With so many festivals out there, how does a filmmaker tell a good one from one that is not so reputable?

Research. Talk to your peers. Start with word-of-mouth from filmmakers who have attended the festival before. Being a new festival in 2011, Napa had the challenge of making sure people knew that, yes, we're a legitimate event, that the accepted films would be shown and seen by an audience. For a festival, filmmakers are your ambassadors in the filmmaking world. So, if hospitality is a priority, and filmmakers are treated like kings and queens, they're going to attend — and they're going to tell their friends. That's really a festival's best calling card.

For new events or if you don't know anyone who's been to a certain festival, evaluate the festival website and press materials. Are they well written and designed or slapped together and full of typos? In the same way you want to present your film well, it's essential for a festival to present itself as professionally as possible. Examining previous programming selections on a festival's website is also a great way to determine if your film would be a good match for the festival."

Okay, I am lucky enough to have my film play NVFF, and I am very excited to attend. What should I do to get the most out of the Festival?

First, provide us with the materials we request to promote and publicize your film — an EPK, film stills, trailer, etc. Even though we are a new festival we have a robust marketing and PR department that wants to tell the world about your film! Make sure you're reading the information sent out from the hospitality department about what the Festival provides and communicate your plans for attending as soon as possible so we can take care of you and make you feel at home in Napa. Communication is key — staying in touch with your point people on the Festival team will help you and your film get the most out of the festival experience.

And then while you're there, network and meet — and all that other stuff?

Definitely! Talk to the audience after your post-screening Q&As, participate in a panel discussion, go to the industry mixer and all the parties! Networking is easy when there's wine involved at most of our events.

Do you have a favorite success story of a film that you screened that got a major boost?

I have high hopes for the narrative film that won both our jury and audience awards the first year of NVFF. One of our jurors absolutely loved it and immediately asked me to put him in touch with the filmmakers because he wanted to introduce them to sales agents and distributors. There's a high likelihood that they're going to get a release beyond the festivals, partly because of having shown in Napa — which is incredibly gratifying.

One of my favorite success stories from past festivals is fabulous and absurd at the same time. I was one of the programmers at what is now the Abu Dhabi Film Festival, but was then the Middle East International Film Festival. It was the first year of the event. I had invited a short animated film that I loved to screen, and at the time, the cultural arm of the government that was underwriting the Festival had the money to fly in all of the filmmakers. So the story starts with this sweet Canadian filmmaker getting to fly out to the UAE and stay at this ridiculously palatial hotel and present his film in a very foreign land.

Before one screening of the animation program, the Festival staff was told that one of the local Sheikhas, the wife of a Sheikh, was planning to go see the films. This is strange enough to begin with; she's practically royalty and she can't sit in the same section with men who are not relations, let alone have a private meeting, so we had balcony seating specifically cordoned off for this kind of occasion. But then, she loved this particular film so much that she asked to meet the filmmaker! I wasn't sure we could even make it happen — she can't sit in the same section as men! But somehow her people worked it out, and they got to sit down and have coffee and talk about his film. It was years ago but I have a completely clear image in my mind of him leaving the Festival later, still shaking his head over the experience. That's one of my favorite stories, just because giving that kind of opportunity to a filmmaker is so fun and, in this case, unpredictable!

I agree — I think that's amazing. Can you describe an incident that you think was a failure, and what steps could you have taken to prevent it — or what have you put in place to make sure that never happens again?

Well, actually at that same festival, we had an excellent documentary that I thought would do really well — it had universal appeal that I felt would really speak to anyone, no matter the cultural differences. Six people attended the film's first screening. And it was in an enormous, opulent theater. It looked bad. I had the job of walking the filmmakers in, apologizing for the size of the crowd, and trying to explain how this could have happened. Thankfully it was a filmmaking team: one was livid, but the other was very levelheaded and understanding. It was a brand new festival, and we learned quickly that much of the local population didn't know what to make of a film festival, or how to participate. The community outreach had not been enough to bring in an audience for a daytime screening of a documentary, even though it was a wonderful film.

What I took away from that experience was that festival programming and marketing/publicity departments have to work together diligently to make sure that the festival's home community knows about the films. You really have to spread the word and make sure everyone knows about screenings: as good as they may be, the films can't simply sell themselves.

What's the nicest thing, or compliment, a filmmaker has ever said to you?

No one instance really pops out — what I appreciate most are those little moments of getting a genuine "thank you" from a filmmaker, of having it acknowledged that you're doing everything that you can to support them and their film. Programmers are in it for the filmmakers, and it's nice to have that recognized.

What's the worst thing anyone has ever said to you?

I think the worst thing — and I need to get a thicker skin and not ever take this personally — but the worst things are when people whose films aren't accepted accuse you of not considering the film thoroughly, of not doing your job, essentially. And that's just an angry person reacting, but it is hurtful when you spend so much time trying to honor the work and honor the process, and give each film its due consideration.

I agree. Do you have a secret blacklist?

Not of specific names, but definitely of behaviors.

Okay, so what are those behaviors?

Occasionally you run into a filmmaker who acts as if theirs is the only film that matters — they demand a tech check at the last minute even if it's going to make a scheduled screening start late, that sort of thing. They don't acknowledge that the festival has a responsibility to our audience and to the other films in the program. It bothers me when filmmakers treat festivals as if they exist to slavishly serve the filmmaker rather than to be a partner in presenting their works. Yes, we are providing a service and we want our filmmaker guests to enjoy the event, but we are looking for them to work with us, to collaborate to show their film to an audience. The filmmaker needs to take an active role and support that effort from their side.

The other behavior guaranteed to land you on my blacklist is treating volunteers poorly. Most festivals rely on an army of volunteers, and they're giving their time and energy because of their passion for the art form, for the event, for the community. For a filmmaker to come in and not recognize and appreciate that upsets me to no end.

If you heard that someone had a horrible reputation from another festival, would that influence your wanting to invite a film?

Inevitably, it would factor in, because how can you possibly set that entirely aside? But I'd like to think that I could separate their behavior from their film enough to make a sound programming decision. I want to consider the film on its merits, and the personality of the filmmaker is secondary. Besides, maybe they had a legitimately bad experience at another festival; it's not fair to assume the worst.

That said, if a film with a reputation like that did get programmed into one of my festivals, I would certainly flag it as a potential "problem" so the festival team is aware of its history and can give that film a little bit of extra attention to make sure we have a smoother experience than the previous festival.

Has your job kind of jaded your opinion of films, or has it expanded your appreciation?

That's a very good question. I can watch films and evaluate from a programming standpoint, and then go see a Hollywood blockbuster and appreciate it for what it is. So I suppose my work has expanded my appreciation and I don't think it has jaded me overall. But my tolerance varies. If I'm in a phase in a programming process where I'm just not seeing anything that I like, it can be tough and it might put me in a funk. You definitely have moments of having to complain to your fellow programmers about all filmmakers doing this, that and the other, and then once you get it out of your system, you go on and see something you love and you're back on track.

If you could give would-be entrants one piece of advice, what would it be?

Well, beyond reading the entry criteria and following those instructions, which we already discussed, learn how to write about your film — it's important that you can describe your work and your story well. It never ceases to amaze me how poorly written, or not compelling, or inaccurate a synopsis might be for a really great film. Run your synopsis by people who have seen your film. Make sure it accurately reflects your work, and if you don't feel like writing is your strength, find someone to write it for you or to edit your draft. Your write-up of your film is an important tool, in both getting it programmed, and then getting it publicized once it is in a festival.

I could not agree with you more. In a catalog I edited last year, of 145 log lines, I had to rewrite 130 of them because they either didn't make sense, had nothing to do with the reality of the film, or had grammar and punctuation flaws. And for synopses, they are either way too long — well beyond the recommended 40 words — or incomprehensible.

And the worst is when it makes you question your evaluation of the film. Like, does this synopsis mean that the filmmaker didn't accomplish what they set out to do? Or does this just mean that they can't describe what they did?

Right, I could not agree with you more. I am not expecting all great directors to be able to write a perfect sentence....

...but you should be able to clearly describe what your film is about. I go into a program book process planning to rewrite as many of the synopses as I can, to tailor them for our audience — and I agonize over them. I really, really try to follow my own guidelines about describing a film because it is so important to your audience, to the people previewing a festival lineup to be able to get an accurate idea of what a film is like. The ultimate goal is to get the right people into the theater so everyone wins: the audience, the filmmakers, and the festival.

Exactly. So finally, what three words best describe what you have to do in a day?

1. Evaluate
2. Curate
3. Connect

"FIND FABULOUS FILMS" CEVIN CATHELL

Former Programming Director, Sonoma International Film Festival, 2007, 2009, 2010, 2011
Former Director, Jackson Hole Film Festival, 2008
Former Director, Santa Barbara International Film Festival, 2005, 2006

About the Festival:

- Founded in 1997, the Sonoma International Film Festival takes pride in showcasing emerging talent, providing a supportive environment for filmmakers, and creating a rich cultural asset for Northern California's wine country.
- 5-day event for general audiences
- Website: sonomafilmfest.org

I met Cevin a few years ago when we spoke at the International Film Festival Summit in Las Vegas. She is funny, wicked smart, and a true believer in telling it as it is. She has an amazing knack for choosing films, which is why she was been called on to program for three iconic festivals. Her background as a film producer has allowed her to see all sides of the business, and affords her an insight that many festival directors simply do not have.

Cevin has been a featured speaker, panelist and juror at a number of film festivals, universities and seminars. She is very encouraged by talented filmmakers and is passionate about bringing their works to enthusiastic audiences.

Cevin, you have an amazing pedigree, having programmed some of the nation's most iconic festivals. Which festival do you want to concentrate on before I ask questions?

I think Sonoma International Film Festival because I was there for five years. I absolutely loved it, and put so much of myself into it. I was saddened to leave in 2011, but my husband was afforded an incredible opportunity — unfortunately, on the opposite coast.

What size is Sonoma right now?

About 1,000 films are submitted and around are 100 selected; one-in-ten. Most come from submissions, and a few come from my travels to the Toronto Film Festival, Sundance Film Festival, Palm Springs, Berlin and various others.

How did you get involved with the event?

While I was the Program Director of the Santa Barbara Festival, the sister of the Executive Director of Sonoma would come down and saw me introducing films, how the Festival was managed, etc. He invited me to come up and check out their festival, and I absolutely loved it. The volunteers were wonderful, the set-up was great, every filmmaker was put up for the entire festival, the food and wine element was incredible — but I thought they needed good films. It was the only area where they were lacking.

The first year they brought me on, 75 filmmakers showed up; last year there were 220 filmmakers in attendance.

What is your background?

I was a film producer in the heyday of independent film making – late 80s to late 90s. I produced films that played film festivals, and one even opened the Toronto International Film Festival.

I did a lot of budget and schedule work for HBO, New Line, Fine Line, Warner Brothers, Paramount and a bunch of TV films.

Before you got into the festival business, did you attend many?

I attended the Santa Barbara Film Festival…that was the only one I went to. However, I was also on the committee that started SXSW. I was a musician in Austin at the time, and along with the Mayor and head of the Chamber of Commerce, they brought in some musicians — and I was one of them. When it became a film festival, I went back to speak on panels and bring my films.

I have also spoken at several universities — Santa Barbara, the Hollywood Seminar that was put on by University of Texas alumni. At that event, the other panelists — some big filmmakers — looked at the audience and told them to all go home — that LA was not the place for them. I was the only person who said I liked my job, and that the challenges were so rewarding.

As a programmer, how many festivals a year did you attend?

Probably about 5 a year. Sundance and Toronto on a regular basis. Palm Springs and San Sebatian in Spain (which was wonderful by the way), Berlin, Mill Valley, San Francisco, Atlanta, SXSW and the Austin Festival, at which I would speak.

Which one was your favorite?

As a film festival professional, Toronto is my favorite because it is organized so nicely and you get to see a lot of films — up to 6 films a day. And the parties are much easier to get into or get invitations to because they are so interested in film festivals. Whereas, at Sundance, they are looking for money and it is harder to get into the parties and other events. Toronto is open and the volunteers are great, plus it is a great time of year. It is so international; the films they bring in are films you won't see anywhere else. They try to cover as many countries as possible, and I have seen pretty raw filmmaking from Turkey and Afghanistan, but it is all so wonderful.

What role does attending other film festivals have in your process?

At other events, I can experience what types of films they are showing, and how audiences relate to them. I also get the chance to talk and catch up with my peers. It gets lonely in your office, and it is good to realize you aren't alone.

On to the main event: Can you describe the selection process at Sonoma?

We go through the Withoutabox system for our applications. When the films come in, there are about fifteen people on the screening committee — many of whom are professionals or have some film experience, and others are just film fanatics, which I like to see because they represent the community. The films are seen twice, and I see every film that comes in.

All 1,000?

Yes. A lot of times I will see them at 2x the speed, because I know what I am looking for and my brain can function that fast when I watch a film. I feel I owe it to the filmmaker to watch the work.

Do you watch them in their entirety?

do if I can.

There is just one committee?

Yes, each film goes to two people on the committee. The ultimate decision is made byme with input from the Board of Directors. I will not put a film in if I think the audience will not like it — even if a large donation is hinging on it.

Did you create this system?

Not really. It was already in place when I arrived. I did, however, make changes to the questions in the rating system. I wanted to get the screeners' opinions and emotions of the stories, including production value, acting, and if they thought others would like it. Even if they hated it, I wanted to know why.

What qualities make a good screening committee member?

While enthusiasm for film is important, I do not want someone who loves everything. That is a killer. People with a discerning eye and different backgrounds is key. Diversity in experience: bankers to fast-food workers.

What is the time frame for judging films?

The submission process goes for four or five months, ending in January, and we have another month before we announce the selections. There is always a flurry of activity trying to talk to filmmakers from Sundance who are trying to get deals for their films, and want us to hold off. But we also need to get the program guide to the printer and the layout has to be done a month before the Festival. It's a tough balancing act.

Did you charge an entry fee?

We did and it was pretty standard for U.S. festivals. The money kept the Festival going until we sold tickets and passes. There were many times I was not paid during this time, because the dollar amount of submission fees is really quite low in relation to the overall budget.

Festivals are going through a tough time financially. Although the budget for Sonoma was $600,000, only $125,000 was cash – the rest was in-kind donations. My salary was halved each year I worked there. I stayed because I loved it.

Where did you publicize the call for entries?

Online, *Filmmaker Magazine*, through local and international filmmaker groups – wherever I could post something. I would also create postcards and bring them to other film festivals.

What are your thoughts about on-line screeners?

I love them. I worked in Sonoma, but I lived in Santa Barbara, so keeping up with the DVDs was difficult. When I could get a link, I could watch it right then and there.

As a matter of policy, does Sonoma give feedback to filmmakers or just an acceptance/rejection letter?

If I went after a film and didn't put it in, I called the filmmaker to say I was sorry we couldn't fit it in. But for everyone else, I sent out a form letter, because a thousand individualized letters was a lot of work. Also, at that point in the process, I was busy with the details of the Festival and couldn't do individual letters. But if a filmmaker contacted me, I always gave them feedback.

Did you find media kits helpful?

I did not find them helpful in the decision making process; I found them very helpful when I was debating between two films.

What is the most important thing for a filmmaker when submitting to a festival?

Submit your film in the official way. I have had a few people call and say, "My film is going to be in the Festival. Where can I send everything?" I think some members on the Board of Directors would ask filmmakers to be in the Festival, and the filmmaker would misinterpret an invitation to submit with an acceptance. Even if you are asked to submit, fill out the forms.

Does Sonoma pay screening fees?

No. In Santa Barbara, we did — but miniscule amounts. I think initially we paid one screening fee last year and that was because we were going to show it in the Latino community of Sonoma and we needed a specific type of film. The distributor who had it would only give it to us with a screening fee. Most of the time, we paid only the cost of shipping.

What kind of jury prizes did Sonoma offer?

The prizes were stock: Best Short, Best Animated, Best Feature, Best Documentary, etc. The last couple of years, I trusted the selection committee enough to give special awards, which they liked to do. Of course, we always had the audience choice awards as well.

Sadly, we did not give cash prizes. We did before the economy tanked. But we awarded computer programs, an editing sound system from THX and Dolby. Everyone received a magnum of wine, and last year, the artist wife of the Executive Director presented each award winner with a painting.

Do you offer travel funds and lodging for filmmakers?

We do not offer travel funds, but do offer lodging for the entire five days. The majority of filmmakers stay in private homes. It is Sonoma, which is wine country, and the homes are beautiful and the hosts are always welcoming. That is why 220 filmmakers attended last year — because they heard about it and they are the talk of the town for the time they are here. There was lots of sobbing on closing night because they had to go back home.

What elements do you think make for a successful film?

Strong story and good acting. Production value is not as important, because it takes a lot of money and that isn't necessarily what I am looking for. I also like to be surprised, and it is hard to surprise me since I have read hundreds of scripts and seen thousands of films.

I personally like quirky films...the quirkier the better. One that comes to mind is a short called *Piñata's Revenge* which is only two minutes long. It is about kids who like to knock over piñatas and then the piñatas get their revenge. It is shot like a 70s movie with the scratches and washed-out look.

What are the red flags that signal a film you want to turn off?

Bad acting or really stilted dialogue. If the dialogue makes you roll your eyes and question if people really speak like that, then the audience will just giggle.

I am not really into gratuitous sex and gore. I think they have their place in film, but if it is only sex for sex's sake, I will probably pass. Usually, it means the director added the scene to see the actress' boobs. And abuse is difficult to program.

Were you influenced by premiere status?

No. I know it is important in getting press coverage, but we always ended up with a great deal of world premieres without looking for them. I don't know why – maybe the films that didn't get into Sundance wanted to play soon after at Sonoma. We did have free wine. We also found that we would often be the first festival that a film played after Sundance.

Were you influenced by accolades that a film might have received at other events?

No, and as a matter of fact, I have turned down many films that have played some of the bigger American festivals because I didn't think they were good enough for us. They may have had some great actor in it, but if it is not a great film, I am not going to show it. There was an instance where I turned down a film that had an Academy Award nomination because the other documentaries we programmed were better.

How important was your audience in the selection process?

Sonoma audiences are pretty open. I wanted them to have an experience they wouldn't get elsewhere. I wanted to expose them to film. Not that I gave them a film that they would love all the time — sometimes, I wanted them to grow to love it.

Did you ever program a film that audiences could not get into?

Yes. There was a Romanian black comedy that I thought was hysterical, *The Death of Mr. Lazarescu* about a man who becomes a non-entity in the state-run health care system. I thought it was great and I laughed! The camera work was right there. Our audiences thought it was too depressing.

How important were the thoughts of your sponsors and donors in your process?

They are very important, and there are times they have wanted to see a specific film or asked that I program a certain type of film for a particular audience. I would not program the film as part of the competition, and instead called the screening a private event. It was not fair to subject the entire audience to a film with a particular slant.

What part did the distributor play in your process?

For foreign features, I needed to go through distributors. Most of the films have some sort of representation, and the distributors can negotiate with us in English. I also have relationships with other distributors, who I will call up and ask if they have an appropriate film. There are some very generous people out there, and they have been incredibly generous to us with great films I do not think would have come to us any other way.

How did you schedule the films in the Festival? How do you choose which one goes in which slot?

I know from the calendar how many films I can fit into a day, and I have several different film sections: international, features, documentaries, shorts, animated, super low budget comedies, local shorts, local films, which I need to find places for. I have to mix shorts up with animated and live action features. If I have better documentaries one year, I will take away narrative feature spots to accommodate them.

Your schedule seems quite fluid.

Again, it is all about the right film for the audience. What is the point of programming mediocre films of one genre when there is an abundance of other great ones?

Did you consult with other film festival directors?

If I am trying to get in touch with a particular filmmaker, I will contact the festival organizer. I also ask around for lists of award winners or audience favorites. Sometimes it is easier to get a screener from another festival than the filmmaker. In my experience, we have been very helpful to each other.

In your area, how many other festivals were there?

Five or six major ones, including Mill Valley Film Festival and the San Francisco Film Festival. Although these events were a few hours away, our audiences travel.

What industry publications do you regularly read?

Variety, Hollywood Reporter, IndieWire, and *Filmmaker Magazine* are regulars. When I am getting a haircut, I will read the trash: *Us, People*, etc.

Was your film festival up for Academy consideration?

I think at various times it was.

Do you think that matters to filmmakers and audiences?

I think it matters to some filmmakers – those who think they have a film worthy of Academy Award nomination – but to most, not really. It was definitely not important for our audiences.

With so many festivals out there, how can a filmmaker tell a good one from a bad one?

Today with the Internet, they should research the filmmaker's point of view: read reviews from filmmakers and audiences who have attended festivals in the past. There is a lot of information out there. Do a lot of research, and do not judge an event on what only one person says.

What should a filmmaker do at a festival to get the most out of their experience at a festival?

Promote your film. Before you even show up, get in touch with publicist for the festival, send clips and introduce yourself. We set up pre-festival interviews with local publications and radio stations, so those who help us get those slots. We also did web feeds which we recorded at the Friday filmmaker gathering. The clips would rotate online all day long. And of course, postcards for those standing in lines — and a few clever filmmakers wear costumes. People remember you!

Do you have a favorite success story about a film that played at your festival?

There are quite a few. I loved the doc *Fat, Sick and Nearly Dead* and had to convince them to let us be the world premiere. I argued that the film would play in a unique environment, and they could use their experience to tweak their strategy for other festivals. The screenings all sold out, and the film has gone on to play at dozens of festivals and hundreds of small screenings.

In Santa Barbara, there was a low-budget musical called *Half Empty* that just tickled my fancy. I knew the executive director at Santa Barbara would hate it because it didn't have any big-name stars and it was kind of rough. But I thought it was my favorite of the Festival, so I kept two slots open, and at last moment inserted the film into the schedule. The film did so well, we added an additional four screenings, and the last two sold out. People were so desperate to get in, they bought tickets for another movie and sneaked into the theater. If the fire department showed up, we would have been shut down.

Conversely, are there any failures you can talk about?

Yes, and I have learned my lesson. There was a local film that wasn't that great, but I wanted to encourage the filmmakers since the film had some promise. Because of the subject and the film quality, there was only one slot I could fit it into — a Saturday night against our big award ceremony. Only 17 people showed. I should have embraced it more and promoted it, but I could only do so much. The filmmakers were local and should have invited everyone they knew. That alone should have filled up the venue.

What is the nicest thing a filmmaker has said to you?

I guess I am incredibly flattered when they ask me to produce their next film.

One year, we screened *The Thing About My Folks* with Paul Reiser and Peter Falk. I did an on stage interview with Paul, which was wildly received. At the end, I mentioned to the audience that it was important to vote for the Audience Choice award — as we did after each film we screened. Maybe it was the talk, or maybe they genuinely loved the film, but it ended up winning the award. The next year, Jeff Dowd [the film's producer] came up to me at Sundance and thanked me — he believed that the award is what helped them get a distribution deal.

What is the worst thing a filmmaker has said to you?

There have been people who have attended the event with much higher expectations than they should have, and ended up being major complainers. I thought they should have sucked it up. It is what it is.

Do you have a blacklist?

I do. I think we all do. It is usually reserved for filmmakers who have treated others badly at the festival. I listen to how people have been treated, and how they have conducted themselves. Like the ones who show up with 25 unticketed friends to a sold-out event and expect paid audience members to be removed for their entourage. No way.

What are some recent trends you see forming in new films?

If the filmmaker is young, there is this trend that a character commits suicide or somehow dies. It gets tiring.

Here is a great trend I see — because technology has gotten so much cheaper and available on devices as convenient as your phone, anyone can make a film. I think people are getting confidence to make short films, which I think is wonderful.

From the point of view of a shorts programmer, I will beg to differ.

Ha ha!

Do you think the proliferation of film schools has made for better films?

I think film schools show people the nuts and bolts, but it is up to the filmmaker to make a compelling movie.

What do you think is more important – schooling or storytelling?

Storytelling because being on the set is the real schooling, anyway.

Do you think you get jaded after a while as a film programmer?

I do not feel jaded. I enjoy film for what it is. I actually feel I can go to a blockbuster film and enjoy it for what it is. I don't take it apart.

If you could give one piece of advice to someone who wanted to enter your film festival, would it be?

Establish relationships with programmers, be humble, treat all film festivals with respect —and go for it.

What three words best describe what you do?

1. Find
2. Fabulous
3. Films

"SELECT. BUILD. PARTY" PATRICK VAN HAUWAERT

Program Director, Razor Reel Fantastic Film Festival (Bruges, Belgium)

About the Festival:

- Founded in 2008, Razor Reel Fantastic Film Festival showcases unique fantastic films to eager audiences, connecting filmmakers with their fans.
- 8-day niche event for audiences who enjoy fantasy, sci-fi, thriller, and horror films.
- Website: RRFFF.be

Frustrated with a French-focused festival in the Flemish-speaking town of Bruges (and yes, it is just as amazing as you see in the Colin Farrell movie), Patrick Van Hauwaert and his friends set out to do something about it.

With no formal training in how to run a festival (he is an IT guy), and fueled by his love of the fantastic film genres (fantasy, sci-fi, thrillers), Patrick and a high school friend have created a week-long showcase that rivals some of the largest in the industry.

How did Razor Reel get its start?

First, you need to know the complicated history of Belgium. There are six separate governments — of which you could live under four simultaneously. To add to the complexity, there are three languages spoken: Flemish, French and German — each of which is a source of pride for the people who speak them. The Brussels International Fantastic Film Festival, our biggest genre festival, which is now thirty years old, focuses almost exclusively on films for a French-speaking audience.

After a couple of years of attending BIFFF, I decided to do one for Flemish-speaking audiences. I called a high school friend of mine, and we hatched the idea to show a day of films in Bruges. Then we started speaking with a well-known Flemish director and film creator, Jan Verheyen, who you might know from a movie called *Little Death*, and he pushed us to do a whole weekend. The first year ended up as a five-day festival with 20 movies.

And your background is not in film?

My background is in IT. I just love film!

Did you attend film festivals before beginning Razor Reel?

Yes, my wife and I love to attend film festivals and we go to festivals in Amsterdam, Rotterdam, and Brussels frequently. Still, the language problem and the lack of a fantastic Flemish film festival is an issue, which was the reason I felt I needed to start a film festival.

At one event, I was sitting at a Q&A session at the BIFFF, and a non-Flemish speaking moderator was trying to interview a Flemish actress in French. It was a small disaster until I got so frustrated, that I ended up translating the questions and answers. That is when I realized that we should have our own.

What is your favorite film festival?

The Rotterdam Film Festival, which is not a fantastic-genre festival. It is very open-minded and programs a full range of films from experimental and niche to general. Plus there is so much to do! There are seven or eight venues, each with a few theaters — so there are about 20 screening rooms showing film from 8:00 a.m. to 2:00 a.m.. And they all have expo halls, live performances, and music in the lobbies. There is so much going on besides film, that the event creates a minor city of its own.

Can you describe the submission and selection process at Razor Reel? How do you get the films? How are the final ones selected?

We publicize a call for entries through our website, mailings, and press releases. Our call is about seven months in advance, and we have another two months after the deadline before we announce the program — so we are working approximately nine months to watch all of the films.

The application form is online, and I have to say, we do not charge a submission fee. This is important, because in the U.S. I know that this is very different.

In Europe, most genre festivals have no fees to enter.

We have a group of screeners that ranges between four and eight people, and we make sure that each film is seen by at least three of them.

Do you watch all of the films in their entirety?

It depends on the movie. Ideally, we watch the whole movie, but if the movie is really bad we stop watching after fifteen minutes.

Fifteen minutes for a feature should give you a good idea about a film.

When a film is really bad in the first few minutes, and does not look like it is going to improve, I am pretty sure that there is no way we would program it. We don't want to bore the audience with it. I trust the three people to make a solid decision. Bottom line: when the three decide that it is crap, we don't show it. If the film gets a "thumbs up" or a "maybe," I send it to other members of the group. For the very difficult ones — the films that don't have a consensus opinion, I make the final vote.

Did you create this system?

Yes. When we first started, I was the sole programmer, which I did not like very much because it was very difficult to make all of those decisions. It was, and still is, a lot of pressure. Over the years, we have added more people to the group. And of course, it evolves every year — we now have a much longer list of criteria we look at (acting, production values, editing, light, sound, and story). At the end of the process, we examine what worked and what didn't so we can improve for the next year.

What qualities make a good screener?

We have many people who apply to be a screener, but the first thing we need to make sure of is that they have enough time to see all the films. We rely so much on their input, so a commitment is key. We have had problems in the past with people who sign on and only watch two to three movies before they are tired and do not want to continue. We look for amateur or semi-professional filmmakers who have knowledge of cinema and love the genre. At this time, none work full-time in the film industry.

Do you take online screeners?

We do, but I am not too happy with them. While many filmmakers are sending links, I still want to watch a movie as I would in a theater…I want to be relaxed, sitting in a big seat with a big screen. I have to watch most online submissions on my computer, and it is not the same experience.

Also, submissions with timed viewing codes have been a problem. Some links only have a five or ten-day expiration, and I often cannot get to a film in that time. Getting new codes is a hassle, and often difficult, since we are screening films in the evening, and it is hard to contact filmmakers after hours.

At the end of your process, do you usually give feedback to filmmakers?

Actually, we don't give much feedback, and I don't feel right with it. I certainly hope that we can improve in the future on this issue.

Do you find media kits helpful when making decisions?

Not in the selection process, but once the movie has been selected, we need the media kit to help with publicity.

What is the biggest mistake a filmmaker can make when submitting a film to a festival?

To be over-confident that the film will be selected. Let's face it, my taste is not your taste, nor is it often that of the filmmaker. The film might be very, very good, but it might not fit in with what we are programming. Filmmakers who have high expectations are often the ones most disappointed.

Do you pay screen fees?

Yes. Unfortunately, we have to. We would rather not, but for many distributors, it is mandatory. Films from Asia are very expensive, and we need to find monies to pay for them. The trick for us is to invite them over and have them as our guest. This is more expensive, but emphasizes our festival atmosphere.

Do you offer jury prizes and what are they?

Last year, we gave awards for the first time for our short program because the Festival is a part of the European Federation of Fantastic Film Festivals. One short film shown at Razor Reel was awarded the Méliès D'Argent. That is then automatically eligible to win the Méliès d'Or award for best European short film.

We also have audience awards, which are appreciation awards. In 2012, we added jury awards and an award for best first- or second-time European feature director.

Can you talk about the European Federation of Fantastic Film Festivals?

The EFFFF consists of 20 festivals in Europe, with supporting members in Asia and the U.S. The idea was started so that together, they could present a major award for a fantastic film, called the Méliès d'Or (after French film pioneer, George Méliès). The organization also promotes fantastic films at film markets and other festivals. The organization started with seven festivals and has grown over the years. We are very proud to be a member of this group.

That is very cool. While we have many groups for festivals in the U.S., none work together to award prizes. Are your programming decisions ever influenced because a film has played at these or other festivals?

For my final decisions: no. But one of the reasons to belong to the EFFFF is to gain access to films you really want to see, but might not be able to get any other way. We often work with a few other festivals to negotiate screening fees for a particular film, or share copies of films. Also, when attending these other festivals, extra effort is made to introduce film directors to festival programmers.

What are your thoughts about the premiere status of a film? Does a world premiere at Razor Reel mean a lot to you?

While we would love to have films with world, European, or Belgian premieres, it is not an imperative. That said, with so many films available on illegal download, we try to make cinema something more rewarding than just watching a film, so we have the actors/directors over to talk about their films.

Are your programming decisions influenced by awards or accolades won at other festivals?

Not always, but it helps to have heard of a film, especially ones with accolades, when coming up with our list to movies to invite to submit. We usually invite some of the award-winners from BIFFF. Thy still have to go through the same selection process as other films.

Are you influenced by famous actors or directors connected with a film?

For myself, no, but I am always thinking about the audience. If you want to attract an audience to your festival — and that is what we all want to do — then a big name helps people make a decision about attending. And once you have them attend your festival, you have to give them reasons to stay — or more importantly — come back.

How important are the thoughts of your sponsors or donors in your decision-making?

They have no say in the kinds of movies we play. They get advertising only and no editorial control.

How important are pressures you might be under from distributors?

We need to work with distributors to go through their catalog of offerings. We must negotiate screening fees, and sometimes travel, for the filmmaker. When a film comes to us without strings, sometimes it is more attractive, since it will cost us less. But it still has to play as well as the other films we select. We are always trying to keep our relationship with distributors happy.

How important are the thoughts of your audience toward your decision-making?

The audience is everything. I need to find films I think will connect with their tastes and likes.

That said, I also have to find the right film for the right theater. We show a special section of art-house or bizarre movies called "Razor's Edge" where I am able to screen films I am not sure if the audience would like. It is a small venue that attracts a smaller, edgier crowd.

Have you ever programmed a film that you loved, but it ended up falling flat with audiences?

Oh yeah! Again, it is about taste, and sometimes I am sucked into a world that I find incredible, but my audience just will not go there for whatever reason. I think that every time it happens, I learn more about my audience, so I am able to better select films for the future.

When you put your final schedule together — fitting films into the various time slots, do you think the schedule influences the types of films you choose? Do you ever have to take out a film or replace it with another to make the schedule fit?

Well, the 10:00 p.m. and midnight screenings are easier to program because we show harder films — which we get plenty of. But in the afternoon, the teenagers show up and we want to screen something appropriate for them. But if we can't get one, we move on and program something else. When selecting a film, I am not really thinking about the programming element.

How many festivals are there in Bruges now?

We have only two, ours and Cinema Novo, which focuses on films from Africa, Asia and South America.

Do you think other festivals in your area are competition or do you work well together?

Actually we all work together and we talk to each other. We even have a program where each festival picks a film that will show at the others' event. We choose an African or Asian genre/fantastic film that they will program, and they do the same for us.

What attracts you to a movie?

Good plot, good score, and good lighting. I like sci-fi and horror, but films with a very dark palette don't work for me.

Also, it depends on the mood you are in at that moment. There are times when I see a film in a theater at another festival and love it. Between the atmosphere of the busy festival and the crowded theaters and smart audiences, the film shines. But when I screen it at home, it isn't the same.

Completely agreed. What makes you want to turn off the DVD player? Do you have any taboos?

In our second year, someone sent in a box with DVD and T-shirts and media kit — everything and then some. But when I put the disc in, it was just so bad. After 10 minutes, I turned it off. Sending me a fancy package does not make up for a poor film.

As for taboos, just the common sense ones: we do not screen kiddie porn, torturing of animals — anything like that. Everything else in context. While we show a lot of horror, unjustified excessive gore is just silly.

For filmmakers who attend Razor Reel, do you offer lodging or travel funds?

Yes. We support filmmakers we invite. For non-European directors, we offer three nights in a hotel and meals, and for Europeans we offer two nights. We also provide transportation to and from the airport and around town. If some directors want to come, on their own initiative, we sometimes negotiate a deal to pay for flights.

Do you offer seminars or panels for filmmakers?

Yes, this year we programmed a full day of seminars for amateur and semi-professional filmmakers.

When a filmmaker attends Razor Reel — or any festival — what should they do to get the most out of the experience?

First, they need to be prepared to talk about every aspect of their film. While they are in Bruges, we often pair filmmakers with the press for interviews, and of course, we have Q&As after the screenings. Be prepared to give autographs and chat with everyone.

Also, since the beer in Belgium is very strong, I suggest you learn your limits ahead of time. Last year, a filmmaker went to the bar during his screening and could not stand up for the Q&A afterwards!

Now I really need to get to Bruges! Do you have a success story of a film that played and did well afterwards as a result of your festival?

In 2010, we showed the Italian film, *Shadow*. We were the first festival to show the film on the mainland. The audience loved it, and thanks to the success at Razor Reel, it was picked up by many festivals. The reps from the EFFFF also agreed, and many of those festivals also programmed the movie.

Can you describe a situation you would consider a failure? And how would you keep it from happening again?

In our second year, we were unable to get a digital print of a movie we really wanted — all they could deliver was a DVD. I am not usually happy with DVDs, and I should have looked at it before we screened it, but time slips by when you are busy, and there are often many chores that go undone before an event. Anyway, the DVD was out of sync: by 10 minutes the audio was slipping from the video, and after 30 minutes, it was so out of sync, we had to stop the film. Embarrassed, I had to explain to the audience that this was

our only copy of a hard-to-get film, and refund the tickets.
Now, I now check all of the films. I know what films are going to what theaters, and I test all of the equipment to make sure this will never happen in the future.

What is the nicest thing a filmmaker has said to you?

We have a guest book that filmmakers can write in, and I love to go back and look at the comments that are made. But when a guest comes and really enjoys themselves, the audience, and the atmosphere, that in itself is a compliment.

What is the worst thing a filmmaker has said to you?

I am lucky that no one has said anything bad to my face. I know I mentioned filmmakers who are over-confident that they will play the Festival. One year, I had filmmakers invite themselves to the Festival who expected me to pay for everything. They were producers of one of the films, and we did not offer them hospitality because their presence offered no benefit to our audience. Our audience wants to meet directors and actors, not producers. They made a big fuss when we refused to pay for their expenses and they threatened to tell others of our poor hospitality. In the end, it worked out, but not without a lot of stress.

What thematic trends or technological trends have you recently seen in the films you are receiving over the past year or two?

We are seeing a lot of *Blair Witch*-styled films — mock-documentary horror and first-person POV angles. More and more filmmakers are getting into CGI, often when it is not necessary and more often, when it does not look good or benefit the story.

And now, everyone thinks they can make a film — Final Cut is only $300 and you can use the HD camera in your phone. Not too long ago, you needed expensive equipment which was a barrier for many filmmakers — but kept a lot of bad ideas from being shot to begin with. Just because you can make a movie doesn't mean you should make a movie.

There's been a proliferation of film schools the world over. Do you see an improvement in the quality of films as a result?

I don't think so.

What is important — film school or the ability to tell a story?

Storytelling. I have seen many filmmakers fresh from school with a degree in hand who can't do what they are supposed to do. Then you have those without formal schooling who can really tell an incredible story. Storytelling is very important. Without it, you have nothing.

Do you think your job as a film festival director has jaded your opinion about films, or do you think it has expanded your knowledge and appreciation?

It has definitely expanded my appreciation of film. I am not only interested in the fantastic genre, but now I have a greater appetite for a variety of films and genres that I am fortunate enough to see which otherwise would never make it to Europe or Belgium.

What three words describe what you do?

1. Select films.
2. Build Audience.
3. Have a good time!

If you could give filmmakers one final piece of advice, what would it be?

Write clearly and type your submission form — and be sure and give an active email address or telephone number. I am a festival director, not a detective.

"STORYTELLER. ACTIVIST. TRANSFORMER." JOHN SCAGLIOTTI

Festival Founder, CineSlam (Vermont's LGBT film festival)
Festival Director, Vermont Bear Film Festival
Organizer, Pride of the Ocean Film Festival
Organizer, Kopkind Grassroots Festival

John Scagliotti is the creator and executive producer of the public television series *In the Life*. The show, developed in 1991, is the first gay and lesbian national series on PBS. The show will be in its 20th year this fall. As a prominent award-winning filmmaker and radio broadcaster, John has created a career steeped in enlightening audiences about the LGBTQ community. CineSlam, a Vermont based film festival that John created, is the brainchild of such intentions. At the Festival, attendees of all sorts can be educated on the everyday life of those they may not otherwise acknowledge or empathize with. The goal is awareness, something John has been raising for several decades. For his devoted work to the LGBTQ community, John was recently awarded an honorary doctorate from Marlboro College.

In addition to CineSlam, John created the Pride of the Ocean Film Festival, the first ever LGBTQ festival run on the high seas. For John, even luxury cruising is lacking without the added bonus of sharing great films.

I met John many years ago when he invited me to his farm for a weekend program to bring filmmakers together to watch and evaluate each others' work, and create lasting friendships. It worked.

John, your hands are in so many projects, you make me look lazy! On top of all of your filmmaking projects, you manage to create and run four events a year. Plus produce films. Plus run a non-profit arts center.

I do CineSlam, I do Kopkind Grassroots Festival, which is a documentary festival, I do the Vermont Bear Film Festival and I do the Pride of the Ocean.

Can you describe the film events? Are they separate or interrelated?

CineSlam has been around for six years. It is programmed for a general audience, with a special target to the LGBT community of southern Vermont, New Hampshire and western Massachusetts.

The Bear Festival is a two-day event for about 200 burly guys every summer. In addition to films, there is a campground and huge pig roast.

Pride of the Ocean is a LGBT festival and filmmaker retreat held on a cruise ship. It is a fabulous experience for everyone — an amazing place for filmmakers, producers, and audience members to connect and relax.

And finally, The Kopkind Grassroots Festival is two public screening evenings of social activism documentaries held at the end of the Center for Independent Documentary and Kopkind film camp we hold at my farm each summer. Here a number of filmmakers learn from one another and build bonds to create future projects together.

All four have some connection. For example, if there's a really good film that plays at CineSlam and it seems it could easily play at Vermont Bear Film Festival, then I'll program it. We always show a couple of CineSlam films on the ship at part of the Pride of the Ocean Festival.

Are the processes for curating and selecting films about the same for all events you do?

We search out films and filmmakers. I publicize the call for entries through emails to filmmakers I know and social networks, and of course our websites. We also hire some PR consultants to help get the word out. For the most part, the "committee" is me, and sometimes, a few friends who weigh in with their opinions.

As I mentioned, entries from one event are often considered for another, and vice versa. Each one has such a unique audience — CineSlam is attended by men and women; Bear Festival is all men; Pride is for those attending the conference on the ship, so that's a mixed audience. Our Grassroots is for general audiences, albeit, mostly activists in the area.

For selecting films for Grassroots, I rely on Suzie Walsh (Director of The Center for Independent Documentary) to help with the selections.

How did you get into creating festivals?

Well, we have to start with the Kopkind Colony. After my partner, Andrew Kopkind, passed away, we created an educational residency program here at the farm to promote writing and the arts. We have year-round programming, including music, a film series, poetry, and a few conferences.

At one of these events, Suzie commented that there should be a film component to our programming. That is how CineSlam began. I located two features, screened them, and the Festival was started. Since then, I have added shorts and other programming. The Bear and Pride events all evolved out of CineSlam: the Bear event to appeal to the local gay male population, which is more bear (burly guys) than twinkie (younger, pretty boys); and the Pride event came out of the desire to bring filmmakers together in another relaxed place like a cruise ship as we were running out of summer weeks to do things at my farm in Vermont.

Honestly, I can't think of a place more removed or relaxing as Kopkind Farm, so the ship must be very chill.

As a documentary filmmaker, I am also an activist. That is why I decided to start the Kopkind Grassroots Film Festival. Especially in an area like southern Vermont, there are not many places to see such films — and a population that really wants to see these films.

I have to admit, you are one of my mentors. Can you talk about your background? How you got into filmmaking and the types of jobs you've had and the films you've made?

I had been making documentary films. I did *Before Stonewall*, and even before that, I had been doing documentaries on radio for many years.

I actually started my media work in radio at WBCN in Boston, which at the time was the number-one rock radio station in town. Since we had such a large audience, I wanted to add a gay element to the programming. This was back in the 1970s, when no one was doing gay anything. The real challenge was being able to figure out programming for young, straight kids that would still attract a gay audience. Eventually, my efforts evolved into a one-hour program called *The Lavender Hour* which was the first gay radio program on commercial radio in America. It was a mix of poetry, disco, sound effects — all kinds of things.

So after seven years there, I got into filmmaking and went to film school at NYU. I continued thinking that my audience would always include gay and lesbian people, so I consciously chose PBS as the major focus for the films I was creating. This led to the creation of the first gay series on PBS, *In The Life*.

That is when the challenge really began, because it wasn't a once-in-a-while program, but an ongoing monthly series. I had to convince program directors to continue programming the show. It was incredibly hard to make the shows' themes fun, interesting and fascinating not only for a gay audience but a straight one. Luckily, I discovered that our growing heterosexual audience was fascinated with what was going on in the gay community and so was I.

But we had to watch how far we could go. While I might like a piece about young lesbians in the Lower East Side getting clitoris rings, I knew that this was not going to play in the average living room where a mother and father were watching with their teenage kids.

That was a defining moment for me. As the Executive Producer, I had to start thinking outside my comfort zone to bring material I thought was very important into the mainstream. The trick was in how to look for interesting ideas that were not necessarily propaganda or the politically correct platform that the gay and lesbian community would want to present.

What do you think are the most important elements that make a successful movie?

Well, the first thing I think about is the idea — the concept. What about it is new? Fresh?

Recently there've been so many transgender films, and a lot of them are very much what I call "Transgender Film 101" because the filmmakers don't often have a sense of history — they haven't seen the evolution of transgender films. Ten years ago, I was watching films about the basics of the transgendered experience. But I am still seeing these films! What is the next step? What is the next concept or what's a good idea that involves transgender situations?

I recently programmed a great transgendered film because it had a unique plot twist — and it seemed like the kind of humorous moments that might happen in my life, happen around my kitchen table. I know my audience will connect with the film, its characters and message, because it is happening to many of us.

I can tell you now, nothing ruins a film more than horrible sound. My hope is that filmmakers really try to get good sound — I think that's very easy to learn. However, what's really difficult is storytelling, and teaching how to tell a story.

After bad sound, bad acting is the next death knell. For some reason, acting in LGBT films is often really bad. I just can't tell you enough. It's one of the things that drives me most crazy. Why did they choose such bad actors? I've seen films that are cheap, don't look so good, and have terrific acting. I'll watch that. I think a lot of times, younger filmmakers cast people who they think are pretty or cute or handsome. But looking good isn't going to deliver the story.

In documentaries, the characters are the people telling the story. The characters have to be bigger than life: they have to be interesting, they have to be somebody that you'd want to sit down with at a dinner table and you find yourself putting your fork down while listening to this person tell a story.

During the beginning years at *In the Life*, the rule was that you could not interview any Executive Director of an organization because they were just going to give you the party line. I just found these people so boring, so we never interviewed them. You could interview someone who's out on the field doing something; you could interview beneficiaries of programs; you could interview almost anyone — except the ED. Executive Directors, once they get into that Executive Director mode and the cameras roll, are very stiff and serious and they tell you what the organization is about and what the mission is — and it turns into a fundraising blurb. In other words, boring.

Who is ultimately at fault for picking bad actors or uninteresting interview subjects?

I think the fault lies with the producer, because they are holding the purse strings. Yes, many times directors choose actors based on availability. Listen, we all know it's hard to make a film. You have to make sure the schedules of 30+ people are in sync for a 20-day shoot. It is hell! And I think that there is a tendency to make choices based on people willing to sit through that hell, so your options of finding good actors aren't always there. But my philosophy has always been — if you can't get good actors or subjects, don't bother making the film.

I learned this the hard way. When I was completing NYU film school, my thesis looked great — but ended up a complete mess. We were the first class to ever shoot 35mm, so the quality of film was great. The lighting, the techno, the sound — everything fantastic! Hell, Oscar winner Ang Lee was the sound man and coveted DP Bobby Bokowski was my cinematographer. And the story was written by Andrew Kopkind and Marcelle Clements of *Esquire, New Yorker*, and *Rolling Stone*! Even the music was by Donald Fagen from Steely Dan. But the directing was for shit. And that was all me. I had no control over the actors. That is when I realized that schools can teach a lot of technical aspects of filmmaking — but the ability to tell a story is innate. And directing is a skill you develop over time, and not learn in a classroom.

Do you think the recent surge in the number of film schools are producing too many filmmakers that don't really have proper or nurtured storytelling abilities?

I don't know. I think some programmers think they do, but I don't think they do.

It takes a different sense to be a good director. I think it's not something you learn in school. It mostly has to come from your life experiences and your ability to translate that into compelling storytelling. If you can explain your daily foibles around the dinner table with friends and all are engrossed, then you pretty much have "it."

I think being in the insular world of film school does not necessarily help with directing. Sometimes, I fear that schools might actually hinder a natural ability. Take Jon Bryant Crawford, for example.

Jon's last short, Foot Soldier, *played at a bunch of festivals, including DC Shorts.*

John's sensibilities come from his upbringing in rural Arkansas, being poor, struggling to get into UCLA. I think all those experiences come out in his directing. He's mature and has a good sense of what he's doing because his life is a little more complicated. I think some fancy suburban kid who just ends up at NYU hasn't had a chance to really experience very much — and it shows in his work.

Take Ang Lee, my NYU schoolmate, as an example. The reason why Ang was able to go on to great success was because he was thrown from Taiwan into the strange world of America, and had to deal with horrible American film students who were all there because they all had money. I think that experience of being an outsider might have given him a unique sense that made him an interesting director. He just had a really wonderful sense of himself. I was very much like him: I was an older gay man in film school; I didn't fit in; and I had a lot more to learn than he did.

So, you've programed festivals, you've programmed conferences, and you've programmed television. What's some advice you would give filmmakers who were sending you unsolicited or blind materials?

What I have found over and over — no matter the genre — is that it comes down to story. If someone has a really interesting story, something really distinctive and interesting, that's the number one thing, for me. If their narrative piece is just the same old story — coming out, getting bullied —

we know that old story, and it's just not enough nowadays.

In documentary it's the same thing: I always ask myself, "Why do a doc on this subject?" If the reason is new and different, then the film has a good chance of being seen.

I just saw yet another film about the gay people taking over a community. The first thing I thought was, "You know, they're missing all the tension and drama in this community because there are white gay people moving into a poor neighborhood, and this is only interesting to the filmmaker." The director never explored the existing community and the impact that gentrification has on the historical population of the area. The real tension — and the reason the film could be interesting — has to do with the history of gentrification: people move into a poor neighborhood, housing prices go up, and long-entrenched residents are forced out. They end up moving to another neighborhood that will, eventually, be targeted again by the next round of gentrification.

That kind of stuff is, to me, really fascinating. But if people aren't willing to engage in those kinds of dramatic stories, then there's no point in doing a community story. You need drama in the documentary. So, what I would say is that the people really need to have an interesting hook.

Is that all?

You know, a lot of people just think that filmmaking is about the dialogue. I couldn't agree less. It's what you do with the camera: how you move the camera, how you go into a room with a camera. Every time you move the camera, it should be telling a story. It should be part of the story, a reason for the story.

Even in documentaries I've found many filmmakers think dialogue is the most important thing. I think what I try to stress in our documentary camps is go look at really good feature films and see what they do with what we call B-Roll. The silliest word we ever created in documentary filmmaking is "B-Roll." It should be called "Focus Roll" because the images you choose should be designed for a purpose and a reason and have thought put behind it — to focus on what the character and interview and world at large is truly about. It is not throw-away footage, but an integral part of the story.

I was watching a really interesting film on older people, and there was a cutaway shot of a plate of spaghetti that I found distracting. The filmmaker should have been asking, "What is the food in terms of the character?" Is the spaghetti something the characters eat all the time? Is it to show the monotony of their lives? Do the strands represent their tangled lives? It was a throw-way shot with no thought behind it, but it was enough to take me out of the picture — and quickly lose interest in the story.

If it's on screen, it should be telling the story. The first rule of editing.

Agreed. So John, as one of my least conventional friends, what three words do you think best describe what you do?

I'm a storyteller. I'm an activist. I'm a transformer.

I think it's very important, whatever the story is, to see another world, see another idea, see another concept that you might not know about, but you feel in the heart, and are better able to understand the plight of others. That's activism.

Even in documentaries, the facts are not very important to me. What's most important is when you finally feel the universal connection between the subject and the visceral, emotional impact — whether it's through humor or pathos — of whatever you're doing. That's transformation.

"CREATE A GREAT EXPERIENCE" JEANNIE ROSHAR

Former Festival Director, LA Comedy Shorts Film Festival

About the Festival:

- Founded in 2008, The LA Comedy Shorts Film Festival and Screenplay Competition is dedicated to introducing the newest and hottest comedic talent to the industry, and helping them make the connections they need to take their careers to the next level.
- 4-day event marketed to film industry insiders
- The festival was shuttered in 2014

Jeannie is a writer, producer, actor, director — and film festival director. Sometimes all at the same time! We met years ago at a conference and instantly connected. Under her direction, LA Comedy Shorts has become one of the major players in comedy film. The industry-oriented festival attracts hundreds of buyers, agents, media producers and filmmakers.

What's the history of the Festival and how'd you get involved with it?

Gary Anthony Williams and I made a comedy short back in 2007. We'd been working together in comedy since 1999, and when we started touring the short around the festival circuit, we were really bummed that the U.S. Comedy Arts (HBO Comedy Festival) had ceased to exist — and nothing had really come through to take its place.

We were tired of playing our comedy in blocks filled with so much drama — there'd be a miscarriage and someone shooting their lover, and you know this horrible thing from the Bosnian war — and then our light-hearted comedy. Needless to say, that didn't sit well with audiences. We wanted to play at a festival that was all comedy, so we decided we would just throw a little weekend at a small theater just for fun. Before the first festival, *The Onion* came on board followed by *Funny or Die*, so we had to book a bigger theater. It outgrew itself even before we started because there was no alternative.

What's your background?

I've been doing comedy in L.A. since 1998. As an actress, as a writer, as a producer and as a director. And Gary, of course, is a fairly well-known actor — and also a director, producer, and writer. So we came strictly from a content-producing background.

And did you have any festival jobs before LACS?

No, but I loved to go to festivals. I thought they were super fun. And of course, like everyone else who starts a festival, I had no idea how much work it would be.

You mean there's work involved? I thought you just put a poster up and people show up?

I mean, we had no idea what we were getting into. Of course, if we did, we probably never would.

How many festivals do you attend now?

It varies year to year. I've gone to Sundance a number of times. We get to a bunch because we do a touring "Best of Festival" program. We tour a 90-minute program around the country to other festivals. It has been screened at Oxford, Connecticut, Friar's Club, Flyway, Trimedia, San Luis Obispo, and a couple of times up in Canada.

So what was your favorite festival (other than LACS), and why?

That's hard because I've attended both as a filmmaker and as a festival director. I will say that the festival most influential to us as we started up was San Diego. We attended as filmmakers and just loved how we were treated. We took a lot of the great things they did for their filmmakers and tried to apply those to our festival as well. They really made the filmmaker feel special.

Can you describe your submission process and selection process?

We take submissions both through our own site and through Withoutabox. Gary, Ryan, and I and now our new partner, Kelly, watch every single film together. We don't pass them off to any subcommittee — we watch every single film. Now, there will be a certain point in our growth where that will be impossible, and we're about at the upper limit. But as of right now, that is the way it is. We watch everything. Together. On the TV, not on a computer.

We watch, we discuss, and then we decide if it should pass on to Round 2. Once we get to Round 2, it's about narrowing down, and fitting things into all of the logistics of the time and space available to us.
It's about seven months from the beginning of the submission process to the date we announce our program.

What changes would you like to make to the system in the future? Or do you think it works for you right now?

It's working right now, and I do love, love, love, the fact that people can submit their screeners online through a link, because I feel like it just saves so much waste. I hated the waste of the paper and the plastic and the DVD — just mountains of trash. I'd love to see that continue and phase out DVDs completely.

Do you charge a submission fee? Why? I don't think filmmakers understand what the submission fees cover.

We're very much a smaller festival. The submission fees go straight to putting on the Festival. I think filmmakers don't realize that the ticket price alone, at least for us, would never even come close to paying for venues, marketing, events and the rest.

Do you give feedback to any of the filmmakers as a matter of practice, or when requested?

As a policy, no. But if someone comes to me — after the Festival, please — and wants feedback, I'll go back and look through the notes and see whatever I can offer them that could be helpful. I do that for the writers, too.

Do you find media kits at all helpful when making decisions?

Nope. They're absolutely unnecessary during the submission process. We don't look at them at all. We don't need them. We don't want them. They end up in the trash, and I feel bad, especially when it seems like it's printed on nice quality paper. I think, "You're wasting your money!"

I know. I agree with you. I don't think too many filmmakers get that at all. I have seen your rules on the web site and it is pretty clear.

I wish filmmakers would read the rules.

Ha ha!

We work hard to word all the rules and all the required materials that are needed — and I feel that so few people read it.

Which leads me to the next thing. What's the biggest mistake a filmmaker can make when submitting film?

I think not following the directions that are laid out for you.

Also we are a comedy festival; if your film is not a comedy, don't waste your money submitting it to us. We get very dramatic films that maybe have one or two moments of levity. I think that's a mistake of beginning filmmakers in believing your film is everything to everybody. Look at it closely. Is it a comedy? If it's a comedy, please submit it. But if it's a dramatic film with a couple funny moments, you should save your money. I mean, I'll take the money, but you should save it for an event that is more appropriate for your film.

Right, because you're looking for funny "Ha ha," not funny "Hmm."

Yeah! And there's plenty of film festivals for those films. I feel bad when I see a good film and it's just not right for us. If it's something I really like, I might recommend them to other festivals.

Do you pay screening fees?

Nope. Never.

Do you have a prize system or offer jury prizes?

We offer a cash prize and a prize package. Last year, the winning film received $2,500 plus an editing package and a music package with a total value of about $15,000. And then for other category winners, we award $500 and some prizes — copies of software and stuff.

Our nine screenwriting finalists are flown in for the Festival and put up in a hotel, as well as receiving cash prizes. We pay for their travel and lodging because that's their way to get exposure at the Festival — it's not like they can screen their script. We want them walking around all weekend talking to people.

Do you offer filmmakers travel or anything like lodging or food?

I wish we could; I would love to. Even so, about 90-95 percent of the filmmakers attend. We get them a good deal on a hotel room, and feed them at parties.

During festival week do you offer panels or discussions?

We do four great panels, which are always a big hit. One is always called "Famous People Talking about Shit," and it's just what it sounds like — it's just like a roast, it's hilarious. And then we have the informative panels on writing, producing in the digital age — whatever we can get great people from Hollywood to speak about, all with a slant on comedy, obviously.

So what elements do you think add up to make a successful short?

For us, it's keeping it only as long as it has to be. Keeping it really short and to the point — and really funny. Those are the most important things. Beyond that, we love something that's original and surprises us and feels inventive; give us something we haven't seen before.

And are there any taboos or red flags — things that you know you can't show?

Being a comedy festival, we probably go a lot further than some others. That said, something that's hateful or just disgusting for the sake of being disgusting would turn me off for sure.

What are your thoughts about premiere status?

I like it, but we don't require it. That might change eventually, but because our festival is for the industry, it hasn't seemed to matter as much.

When you're making decisions, are you influenced by the awards a film has gotten at another event?

No! Not only that, I wish they wouldn't tell me! If someone tells me, "I've won 25 awards from all these film festivals," it doesn't make me feel like I should want it — it makes me feel like the film's kind of been used up. You might have won those awards, but keep quiet, and let me feel like I'm kind of discovering it.

Are you influenced by big names in films?

When I see big names in a film, I have hope that it's going to be quality. And let's face it, big names help us attract press, which helps everyone at the Festival. I've turned down plenty of films with huge names, it makes me sad to do it —but we're not going to screen it if it's not up to our standards.

Obviously, since you're an industry festival, your audience is really important. Do you take their needs into consideration when you're selecting films?

We use the mantra, "Is this is a film the industry should see? That they think people should see? Will they find it funny?" That pretty much guides our thoughts.

Have you ever programmed a film that you personally loved, that the audience just found to be mediocre?

There are always a few films a year that didn't get the response that we thought they would. We just put those notes in the back of our minds and think about that in the next year.

How important are the thoughts of donors or sponsors in your process?

If someone already is sponsoring our festival, they've already signed onto our marketing images of a fat guy in tiny short pants. They know they're signing onto a crazy festival. They have yet to ask us about our programming decisions — and probably never will.

How do you plan your schedule — putting films together in the 10 different blocks? Is it based on theme, topic, niche?

We have some fun when we put them all together. We look for really stupid themes to group them, like "Cops and Robots" or "Quit Bugging Me, I'm Eating Ribs!" We come up with a ridiculous way of stringing films together that is maybe more for our benefit than anyone else's.

So after you put all of your "Rib" movies together and find that the running time is too long, do you start editing the lineup, maybe remove a film, or replace a longer one with some shorter films?

We move things around within the blocks until it works. But, if we love a film, we find a way to make it fit.

Do you curate films from other festivals?

We don't curate, but we might see a film at another festival and encourage the filmmaker to submit. They still have to go through the same process as anyone else.

We definitely like to collaborate with other festivals, and love doing our tour at other festivals. I think that because we are so niche, that we offer something different than other festivals.

Can you talk about the traveling show? It is really unique — and is at the beginning of a trend I see other festivals trying to implement.

Festival programmers tell me over and over that they feel like they don't get enough quality comedy shorts to make a strong comedy block. Therefore, it made sense for us to put together this traveling 90-minute program. It's branded under LA Comedy Shorts and gets our name out there — and they get a pre-programmed block of comedy films. The filmmakers love it, because their film is screened all over the country.

What do you think is more important: schooling, or storytelling?

Storytelling. No question.

What industry pubs or web sites do you read? Do you think they are important in selecting films?

I read *Hollywood Reporter, Variety,* and a few others. It's important for us to know who is looking for new talent — and that's pretty much everyone. Short-form comedy on the Internet has become more and more influential, leading to more and more opportunities. You see Fox and NBC and others doing their own original content for the web. We are the connector between these guys and the filmmakers.

When a filmmaker attends your film festival, what should they do to get the most out of the experience?

They should attend as many events as possible. We only put on one event at a time because we want everyone in the same room at all times. We want everyone together. Our parties are structured in a way that keeps people talking and networking. So just being present, wearing their badge and talking to people is what they need to do.

Do you have a favorite success story of a film that showed at LACS?

Eleven filmmakers — that I know about — have gotten development deals from attending the Festival. And in addition, many have been given the opportunity to screen their films on Comedy Central. So, it's not like one film has gone on and achieved this great glory. I am very proud that we can create opportunities for every film and writer at the Festival.

That's amazing! Can you describe an incident that you would consider less than successful?

I think my less successful moments have come more from having an open bar for too long of a period before the awards ceremony. The first time we had the awards ceremony, we tried showing all the films — and we had also had an open bar, so people just were chatting, chatting, chatting. It was more of a party atmosphere than a screening, and in the end, was not respectful to the films and filmmakers.

What's the nicest thing or compliment a filmmaker has ever said to you?

That attending LACS has been a game changer for them and their career.

What's the worst thing a filmmaker has said to you?

I've never had a filmmaker accepted into the Festival say a bad thing to me. For those who did not play the Festival, I've heard that I don't know what I'm doing, that I have no business being in comedy —or I didn't accept their film because I'm trying to steal their idea.

Do you have a secret blacklist?

We have had one or two filmmakers that threatened us with lawyers because we didn't take their films. They're not worth the liability to me, and I would rather not have their money in the future.

If you hear from another filmmaker or festival director that someone is a diva or high-maintenance, does that affect what you think about their film or whether you want to bring them in?

If I heard a horror story about them, yeah, it would affect my attitude. We work so hard and make so little; no one at the Festival is even on payroll. We're just trying to make it a good experience, and we want people who will appreciate that.

What are some of the trends recently seen with the submissions you've received?

Films made on the cheap. People can make the film on their cell phone and computer, so it's open to everyone. The Internet has also lowered the standards of quality — most of the super-short comedy content looks like it was filmed in 10 minutes with $10. Not that we don't like that — we get a lot of those videos and they are perfect for some of our sponsors, such as Funny or Die or Atomic Wedgie. In the end, I love films that look and sound great, but if it is really funny and original and the quality just happens to be less, we'll still play it.

Do you think that's a different category altogether? Internet content versus Short Film?

I think there can be some crossover. I think your cat falling off the DVD player is definitely an Internet video. Beyond that, comedy music videos that are definitely a great fit in both places. We still look for stories that have a beginning, middle, and end.

Do you think the recent proliferation of film schools has affected the quality of films you're seeing?

I think it affects the technical quality — it's usually higher. But what I don't like is, sometimes, they have a 15-minute thesis film that maybe should be only 11-minute festival film. So I always encourage students to do their project — and when they're done with the school cut, look at how long this film should really be for audiences.

I agree with you! Just because a professor says you can make a film up to twenty minutes, doesn't mean you should make a twenty minute film. Has your job jaded your opinion on film, or do you think it's expanded your knowledge or appreciation of the medium?

I love just watching films that other people make that I never would have thought of. I already was a filmmaker, but being a festival director has been a huge education. Knowing what I know now, I would go back and re-edit every old film of mine.

If you could give would-be entrants one piece of advice, what would it be?

First, show your film to your family and your best friends. They're going to tell you that they loved it and you did a great job. Then show it to some people you can trust to give you honest feedback. And however long your film currently is, you can probably cut two minutes off. In the case of a one-minute film, you probably shouldn't cut two minutes out.

What three words best describe what you do?

How about four? Create a great experience.

"WATCH. PLAN. PARTY." TALLGRASS FILM FESTIVAL

Lela Meadow-Conner, Executive Director
Gretchen Mitchell, Co-Director of Programming

About the Festival:

- Founded in 2003, the Tallgrass Film Festival is the heartland's premier film association. TFF fosters an appreciation of the cinematic arts by creating shared experiences around the international medium of film.
- 4-day event for general audiences
- Website: tallgrassfilmfest.com

Ten years have passed since the creation of the Tallgrass Film Festival and executive director Lela Meadow-Conner and co-director and programmer Gretchen Mitchell could not be more pleased with its progress. The Festival has become one of the largest independent film festivals in Kansas, showcasing over 100 films from every corner of the globe.

The festival's independent reputation only increased after losing the city's sole theater chain as a major sponsor and venue six years in. Lela, her board and staff, did not see this as a setback, but as a chance for growth without limits. The festival took on new (old, forgotten theaters) and even unconventional venues, and eventually, Lela even relocated her household to the city to continue her passion of working for the festival. Lela studied Radio/TV/Film at California State University and met Tallgrass founder Timothy Gruver in Los Angeles. Her background in the entertainment industry includes stints in film and television production, talent management, movie marketing and public relations. (In between festivals she also earned a degree in the culinary arts, to fall back on.)

In the summer of 2005, during a Tallgrass-sponsored filmmaking class, Gretchen Mitchell met Timothy Gruver. This chance meeting would change Gretchen's future endeavors for good. Once a high-school English teacher and journalism instructor, Gretchen chose to join the Tallgrass team, which flourishes in showcasing independent films to an eager audience. Working her day job as a Technical Writer/Marketing Coordinator for an engineering firm in

Wichita, Gretchen has continued her involvement within the Festival working on Hospitality and Programming for the past seven years.

What is the history of Tallgrass?

LELA: The festival was founded in 2003 by Tim Gruver who, after working at the LA Film Festival and Outfest, moved back to Wichita and thought, "I want to start a film festival here." A lot of people looked at him and thought it was ridiculous, but within a matter of months he had secured a really amazing board of directors consisting of arts benefactors, local business people and very well connected people. He then secured a major theater chain in town as a sponsor, and they were with us for the first five years. Sadly, in 2005, right before the third festival, Tim passed away. That year, we shortened the festival to a single day and called it Shortgrass. By the next year, we were back on our feet, due to our amazing staff, board and community, and have thrived ever since.

How did both of you get involved?

LELA: Tim called me and said, "Come to Kansas!" I had never been here before, so I did and now I live here. I know, crazy.

GRETCHEN: I was always interested in film and I had the opportunity to help with craft services for a local film production — and have been involved ever since.

LELA: And from there she became the director of programming.

I completely understand. One chooses the lunch meat; the other chooses the films. Do either of you have film or festival backgrounds?

LELA: I studied radio/TV/film at Cal State Northridge and worked in Hollywood, where in my last job, I produced movie trailers. Before that, I did all sorts of things, from talent manager to producer for a cable channel series.

GRETCHEN: I was an English teacher and right now, my full-time gig is as a tech writer for an engineering firm. I started with Tallgrass volunteering with hospitality, then I worked with the programming crew until I worked my way up to the co-director of programming.

Before you became involved with Tallgrass, were you a regular at other festivals?

LELA: I went to Sundance and a bunch of west coast festivals, and this year I'm going to Gothenburg International Film Festival in Sweden and Seattle International, among others.

GRETCHEN: I have only been to Cannes but others on staff have been to Tribeca, SXSW, Seattle, New York Film Festival and Sedona.

What other festivals do you admire, and why?

LELA: Seattle (SIFF) is really a great event, and I admire everything they do year round there, too. I think there's a lot to learn from attending and watching Tribeca. I also think Telluride is instructive. That is the sort of festival we achieve to be.

Wow, that's ambitious! It's such a different type of festival.

LELA: Exactly. Telluride was never meant to be a competition festival. Instead, it is very much an audience event that attracts quite a bit of industry attention. We are never going to be one of the major industry festivals or markets, but our festival serves the audiences here very well. We are in the exact center of America, and I think a lot of people don't realize the connections that are here. Wichita is a small town, but it's also a very wealthy town.

GRETCHEN: And the buzz that is created here spreads really quickly. It's the epicenter of the country.

Can you describe Tallgrass' submission and selection process in detail?

GRETCHEN: We have about 40 programmers. About 20 are pre-screeners and 20 are actually what we call "programmers." First, each film is watched by three pre-screeners who vote "yes" or "no" and write up their comments. If it passes that process, the film goes to the programming committee where they grade it on a whole cadre of criteria, as well as write detailed comments. From there, all of the comments and scores are read carefully and reviewed. At this point, we start to look at film categories, balancing subject matter, and consider our audience to create a well-balanced program. We invite the ones that rise to the top to participate in the Festival.

LELA: When we say three people watch, the truth is the top selections, and films that need more eyes, are watched by our senior programming committee, who makes the final decisions. They will trade emails and phone calls back and forth for some time to discuss a film's merit.

GRETCHEN: And we talk about all kinds of stuff at that time: our markets, our audience, the film's relevance.

Did you guys create this system?

GRETCHEN: I did. It's an all-online system; the screeners score online and make their comments online.

Do you give those comments back to filmmakers?

GRETCHEN: If they ask for them, we do anonymously.

Of the 40 screeners, what percentage of screeners are film professionals?

LELA: I would say about five to ten percent. But we have lots of programmers who go to various festivals every year including SXSW, Sedona and Telluride.

So it's mostly an audience-driven festival?

GRETCHEN: Absolutely.

What qualities do you think make a good screening committee member?

GRETCHEN: Love of film and storytelling, a discerning eye, and a pulse on the community.

What qualities do you think become a problem with screeners?

GRETCHEN: We warn them about this when we're training — they can't just think about their own personal niches. It's not about whether you like the film subject, but if there is an audience that would like it. You've got to think of the audience as a whole, not just your personal likes and dislikes.
LELA: And the screeners that like everything. You can't get honest feedback from someone who likes it all — there is no variety in their opinion.

You're far from the first person to say that. Screeners who like everything can't objectively score anything.

GRETCHEN: And you know which ones they are — the ones who like them all — and then there are the ones who don't like anything. We just have to account for their scores and rethink their involvement in the future.

And how long is the process to submit and select films?

GRETCHEN: I was just counting that out and it's about eight months for submissions, plus another six to eight weeks before we announce the lineup.

Can you talk about why submission fees are charged?

LELA: To help balance our budget. Basically the submission fees pay for our Withoutabox subscription, and that's about it.

I've heard that from others; the fees you collect through Withoutabox barely pay for their services.

LELA: Yes, barely. And if you want any of their marketing services, the price becomes much higher.

Where do you publicize your call for entries?

LELA: On Withoutabox, our website, newsletters, and cross marketing with other film related organizations.

GRETCHEN: And we send out a press release to industry and media. Facebook and social media are always good — and free. We generally do not pay to list our call — it's mostly just word of mouth.

What are your thoughts about using online screeners?

GRETCHEN: They were new to us last year (2011). We just advertised that we would accept them this year. Last year, we only had a handful. We weren't quite sure how to handle them. We have worked through that for this year. There are definitely pros and cons. It is great to be able to quickly share a film with a sponsor or other screeners. But files that come with time limits are a problem. It is not always possible for everyone who needs to see the film to watch it before the URL expires.

LELA: Personally, I liked them because I could watch films on my own time, as long as there's no time limit. I can watch at home, in bed, whenever.

GRETCHEN: And just not having to make copies of DVDs for screeners is a major time saver.

Did you find any other issues? I know that I'm finding issues with subtitles on online screeners. Many are too small, and after the film is compressed for streaming, I can't read them.

GRETCHEN: We held group screenings last year and projected the films, so that was not really an issue for us.

Do you receive many foreign films?

GRETCHEN: Yes! It's my favorite genre.

LELA: We show a lot of foreign film. I'd say about half our feature programming is foreign film.

GRETCHEN: Our audience won't get the chance to watch these films unless we bring them here.

Do you find media kits useful in the decision-making process?

BOTH: No, not really.

Do you keep them, or do you throw them away?

GRETCHEN: I won't show them to the programmers. Physical media kits seem like a great expense that is usually ignored. We prefer the online media kits. They are "greener." We really don't refer to them unless the committee is really undecided and needs more information or if the film is selected and we need the information for marketing.

What I do think is important is a good cover letter. A well-written letter often gives me more information than a media kit does.
LELA: I find it irritating when a film doesn't have a website with media information and/or a Facebook page. After we make our selections, it is really helpful to have a place where we can easily download information, link to, and share.

What's the biggest mistake a filmmaker can make when submitting?

GRETCHEN: Not sending us enough copies. You should always submit more than one copy of your disc. We've had so many dead on arrival, it's not even funny.

LELA: And marking the disk with all of the pertinent information. So many times, filmmakers don't even have the running time of the film on the label. Which means I have to do a web search to hopefully find this basic information.

GRETCHEN: And most film websites forget to include the basic and technical information that is important to us like the runtime, languages, available formats, etc.

Do you pay screening fees?

GRETCHEN: We do for some foreign films, especially if we are working with a distributor. If it's domestic, we don't. We try to provide travel and accommodations for the filmmaker from that film to attend the Festival instead.

Does Tallgrass present jury prizes?

GRETCHEN: We do not have jury prizes, but we do have other awards. The audience awards, which are our biggest awards, are given for best feature documentary, best feature narrative and best short. And then we have a programming award, which is our answer to a jury award. There are three programming directors, and we choose the outstanding narrative feature and the outstanding narrative doc for the festival. We will be adding a few more awards to the roster this year.

Do you offer hospitality or travel funds for visiting filmmakers?

LELA: Our general rule is that if your feature film is accepted, we try to fly the filmmaker out. We have a budget for one person from each domestic film to attend. We also put them up and provide ground transportation. They're taken care of pretty well, as they should be. The filmmakers are the stars of the show at Tallgrass.

What elements do you think add up to make a successful film?

GRETCHEN: Story, credible dialogue, believable acting, good sound, and there has to be really good editing.

LELA: I will add production value and length.

Are there certain conventions or genres you instantly fall for?

LELA: I love documentary, and finding those is never a problem. I do have to say what always gets my attention is a well done comedy, because many indie films have a darker bent to them, and it can be difficult to find a good, funny comedy. Finding quality domestic film without distribution is tough, but finding a light comedy can be harder.

GRETCHEN: Agreed. While I think our audiences really appreciate the drawn-out bleak films, especially in these times, they really want a good comedy.

What are some of your red flags or taboos that instantly make you think, "I can't possibly program this?"

GRETCHEN: The first thing that comes to mind are voiceovers, because, a lot of times, they are so horrible. Many filmmakers add the VO because they don't have good sound, and so they're compensating for that. I've also seen filmmakers use VO when it really doesn't lend itself to the story.

LELA: I hate, hate, hate, credits at the beginning of a short film. I mean, come on.

GRETCHEN: Or, it's bad sound and bad lighting — or yet another zombie horror film.

Are there any taboos or topics that are completely off-limits?

GRETCHEN: Not for us, not really. We're pretty open. We've shown some freaky films.

What are your thoughts about premiere status?

GRETCHEN: We have gone back and forth on this for a long time. What does a premiere status really mean to an audience? It is probably more important to us (the programming staff) and I think our job is to serve our audience. If that means providing a Wichita screening of a film that's already played in Kansas City or Lawrence, then so be it.

LELA: It has to be a Wichita premiere — that's the bottom line.

Are you influenced by awards or accolades a film received elsewhere?

GRETCHEN: We might be influenced to invite it, but it really does not influence whether or not we decide to have it for the Festival.

What about big names? Does star power influence your decision?

GRETCHEN: We may look at a film twice, or give it more consideration if it has a big name on it, but it still has to be good.

LELA: And just because a film has a big names does not mean it is going to be a gala film or even an official selection. Last year, we showed *The Sandman*. We chose it for our opening film because it is so "indie." We had our choice of bigger profile films with "names," but in the end, decided to go with the one we thought would resonate with our audience.

So, how important is your audience in your final selection process?

LELA: I think it's pretty much the bottom line.

GRETCHEN: They are our main consideration. That said, we also want to broaden our audience's horizons, so we're also going to be testing, or pushing them to see things that they wouldn't normally go see.

Have you ever programmed a film that you loved, but that audiences were just like "meh"? What did you learn from that?

GRETCHEN: We showed *We Are What We Are*, and I thought that would really play well. I was dead wrong — no pun intended. The audience that showed up responded well to it, but audience attendance was poor. I'm not sure if you learn from the experience — it was a great film.

LELA: I mean, the film was such a different genre from what we usually play, we thought it would be well received. But, not as much as we'd hoped. That will happen. It just serves as a good reminder sometimes that we're programming the festival for our community, not for ourselves!

Are you ever influenced by your sponsors or your donors to take a film?

GRETCHEN: They have no say in the selection, but the opportunity for a movie that lends itself to pair with a sponsor is worth considering, maybe a little heavier than another film.

LELA: A couple of years ago, we showed *Twisted: A Balloonamentary*, a documentary about balloon twisting. Well, Pioneer Balloon is based here, so we thought it was a perfect marriage. The film was well received, and a new sponsor was very happy.

GRETCHEN: But we would not let a sponsor or donor choose a film. Or if they recommended one and the film was not up to our standards, we would have to pass on it.

What role do distributors play? Do they have any influence?

GRETCHEN: If we can get a film we want through a distributor with little hassle, we will program it. If they won't let us have it, we'll forget it.

And when you schedule your films, is it thematic, is it by audience, this audience goes to this venue, or what?

GRETCHEN: We try to do a little of that. We lay all of the films out and then decide, "this person might want to see that movie — and might also want to see this movie," and we start to sort them. We also group "like" films together — LGBT, special audiences, etc. We purposely program some films opposite each other. We'll show something serious such as a documentary against a funny comedy in the same time slot.

Do you find that your programming structure affects the type of films you take? Do you ever have to jettison a film because it doesn't fit into the schedule, or you choose another film because it's ten minutes shorter, and therefore it schedules better?

GRETCHEN: I don't think the schedule limits us as much as we are looking for a balance — to attract different types of audiences that will come to the event.

LELA: And a balance of categories and genres to expose as many people to as many varieties of film as possible.

GRETCHEN: However, that being said, shorter films are easier to schedule.

When you visit other festivals, are you always thinking of what you want to program from their event?

GRETCHEN: We have programmers that attend different festivals, and they are always scouting for new films to invite.

LELA: Absolutely – especially at the international festivals. We also scour catalogs from a bunch of other festivals to see what they are showing. It helps us look at trends.

GRETCHEN: We also have relationships with programmers at other festivals, so we are always sharing information. I am more apt to take a look at a film that is recommended by someone I trust.

What do you think is more important, schooling or storytelling?

BOTH: Storytelling!

What websites and industry pubs do you read regularly?

LELA: *Deadline Hollywood, IndieWire, Variety, IMDB, Movieline, Salon, New York Magazine, Vulture, Huffington Post, Rotten Tomatoes,* and honestly, I get a lot of information from Facebook — there are so many, it's hard to keep up.

And you find that important because it gives you a pulse of what else is going on?

GRETCHEN: It gives us a pulse of what else is going on, and keeps us in tune with pop culture. We do a lot with Facebook and other sites. The goal is not necessarily to promote us, but to see what is going on in the indie filmmaking world. We do a lot of scouring just to find out what's going on.

Is your festival approved for academy consideration?

LELA: No. We've started talking about going after accreditation once we get past year ten. Ten years is a milestone: it adds a lot of legitimacy to the event. We did, however, get an AMPAS [Academy of Motion Picture Arts and Sciences] grant last year.

Do you think that academy consideration matters to filmmakers or audiences?

GRETCHEN: I don't think it matters to audiences, but I think it totally matters to filmmakers. There's a category of filmmakers that it really matters to who only submit to the festivals with it. I think we could get more submissions if we had it.

LELA: Yes, clearly we would get more submissions. But I don't think it's first and foremost on the mind of every filmmaker. Or is it?

With so many festivals out there, what steps can a filmmaker take to tell a good one, or a legitimate one, from a bad one?

GRETCHEN: I think the biggest thing to do is the research. Is their website complete and functional? Do they have strong social networking? Do they have a presence on the web, or are blogged about by other filmmakers? Of course, these are generalities — I've seen a lot of festival websites that don't look professional at all — and they are major players.

LELA: I also think that word of mouth is important. At the end of the day, filmmakers who come here are not only ambassadors for the Festival, but for the city. That buzz spreads, and anyone who is looking into us will be able to find that very easily.

So what about Tallgrass is different from other festivals that filmmakers should apply to you as opposed to someone else?

LELA: One of the filmmakers came out and wrote an article for the *Boston Globe* about Wichita from his experience here — it's not what you expect in the middle of the Kansas prairie. I think one of the things that always sets us apart is our audience. They are completely receptive and they're not jaded at all – there's no agenda other than to experience a great film. They're interested in indie film, they're open, and they're willing to try new things. They are eager to take the time to talk to filmmakers, form new friendships with them, and discuss their films. If your film plays at Tallgrass, you're really going to find out what someone in middle America thinks of your film. That's important because at the end of the day, you want distribution or you want to make money on your film and, the coasts are great, but this is the rest of the country.

GRETCHEN: I wonder about filmmakers who say "Oh, I'm done with my festival circuit and I don't want to do the Midwest." It's so important to get the word of mouth out about your film. And people from middle America definitely talk about what they see — and are eager to tell a bunch of people, "rent that one, or go see that one." I always kind of cringe a little when filmmakers are all jaded about doing too many festivals. I'm thinking that's really selling their film short when they should really be reaching all audiences.

What should a filmmaker do to get the most out of the Festival?

LELA: Come to our parties! Come and network, because there are hundreds of millionaires in this city — and few people asking them for film investments. We always say, you might find your next executive producer just by chatting to the person who sat next to you at Tallgrass.

GRETCHEN: Not only that, but people come here and think, "Oh, I could totally film here!" Wichita is an easy city to shoot in — lots of interesting buildings and settings, and you don't need permits to shoot in public areas. I think that there's a lot that can be taken from visiting here, and the biggest is the people.

Do you have a favorite success story of a film that played there and went on to do really well, or anything?

GRETCHEN: I think the first year of the Festival, we had some really obscure film and we thought nobody was going to show up, but at 9:00 a.m. — the theater was filled!

LELA: I know it sounds corny, but I feel really proud of any film that we've screened at Tallgrass, and even more so when they go on to do great things like get distribution, win awards, end up on Netflix and so on.

Do you have a story of a failure or some sequence of events that didn't go nearly as well planned? What did you learn from it?

GRETCHEN: In my mind, it would be tech issues. Not a complete equipment failure, but sometimes filmmakers are very critical of the projection. We now pay a lot more attention to tech issues and make sure that when appropriate, filmmakers have the ability to attend tech checks and see the theater. At the end of the day we want happy filmmakers.

LELA: One year, we had Gary Busey, and Jose Canseco and Cloris Leachman opening their films at the same time. It was pretty much the perfect storm.

What's the nicest thing a filmmaker ever said to you?

LELA: Honestly, I think the nicest thing is when someone gives you a heartfelt hug before they leave, then stay in contact through Facebook or calls. Creating lasting relationships is such an unexpected and appreciated reward.

And what's the worst thing a filmmaker ever said to you, whether they were in the Festival or rejected?

GRETCHEN: I can't think of a single incident, but some filmmakers can be very diva-like. The whole attitude of entitlement or thinking "I'm better than these other people" can be very grating — and wear out a visit very quickly.

LELA: We once had someone question our awards. It was very distasteful.

And do you have a secret blacklist?

LELA: No. But there are a couple filmmakers who I would be really hesitant to work with again. So does that mean yes?

What trends — technological, thematic, story — are you seeing with the most recent films submitted to you? Are the trends welcome?

GRETCHEN: Well, vampire movies. Filmmakers who are just starting out seem to think the zombie movie is the easiest thing to create, so they throw one together. The problem is that they are rarely clever or original.

LELA: And CGI. There is a trend using CGI because it is cool, even though it might add nothing — or worse, take away — from the story.

GRETCHEN: And length. Edit, edit, edit.

How do you see the impact of technology on the quality of films that you are receiving?

GRETCHEN: We're seeing amazing quality compared to what we used to get.

What about the quality of storytelling?

GRETCHEN: Generally it's about the same. But since it is really the most important aspect, it doesn't really matter if the technological execution is perfect, if the storytelling is awful or the dialogue is flat.

What about the proliferation of film schools? Do you think that they are adding more inventory that's mediocre, or is it actually helping to produce solid filmmakers?

GRETCHEN: You know, we have gotten some great student films. We don't have a special category for them, so they have to compete with the regular films. Some do, and some don't.

LELA: We've had some amazing animated films come though film schools.

Has your job jaded your opinion of film, or has it expanded your appreciation of the medium?

GRETCHEN: It has totally jaded me. Nobody wants to go see a movie with me.

LELA: I think it can be hard when you're seeing so many films all the time. Sometimes it makes me just want to go sit in a dark movie theater by myself and watch a fluffy, vapid Hollywood-style movie. But when I see that gem, that is just riveting, it really reminds of why I love movies and I love my job. At the end of the day, we are critics for our community. It is our job to curate the best possible program we can for our audiences.

Do you think that affects your attitudes when watching submissions?

GRETCHEN: If the decision was mine alone, I would say yes. But since we are always thinking of our audience and what they want to see, those considerations overtake personal feelings.

If you could give would-be entrants one piece of advice, what would it be?

GRETCHEN: Edit. Every single review that was written last year by the screening committee mentioned that the films were too long for the plot to support. Short or feature — it didn't matter.

What three words best describe what each of you do?

GRETCHEN:

1. Watch
2. Plan
3. Party

LELA:

1. Plan
2. Watch
3. Party

GRETCHEN: When you're planning a film festival, and everybody's working so hard for no money, you have to have fun. Otherwise, what's the point? No one's being paid millions of dollars here.

LELA: If they are paid at all. Festivals are a labor of love, no?

"THE FILM HISTORY BUSINESS" RICHARD PEÑA

Former Program Director of the Film Society of Lincoln Center
Former Chairman of the Selection Committee for the New York Film Festival.

About the Festival:

- Founded in 1963 to celebrate American and international cinema, to recognize and support new filmmakers, and to enhance awareness, accessibility and understanding of the art among a broad and diverse film-going audience.
- 17-day regional event for general audiences
- Website: filmlinc.com

The annual New York Film Festival is produced by the Film Society of Lincoln Center and to this day remains a highly regarded pioneer among film institutions. Among the numerous talents discovered by the society: R.W. Fassbinder, Bernardo Bertolucci, Martin Scorsese and Wes Anderson. The society prides itself on its influence and ability to discover genuine filmmakers.

Richard Peña, a graduate of Harvard and MIT, has the privilege of showcasing deserving works of achievement in film within the New York Film Festival. As Program Director for the Festival, Peña's influence has made it possible for many international and foreign language films to debut in the competitive U.S. film market. With Richard's guidance and expertise, the Festival has become synonymous with the best in world cinema.

The New York Film Festival is one of the oldest in the country — and one of the most successful, as you are entering your 50th year in 2012. How did you get involved with the Festival?

In 1987, when Lincoln Center was beginning to construct what would be the Walter Reade Theater, I was working in Chicago at the Art Institute. Joanne Koch, the Executive Director, contacted me and said, "We like what you've been doing in Chicago. We're opening our own movie theater here, and would you consider coming to New York?" That was always my dream — to work for the Film Society, so I said, "Yes. I'd love to come." So I did, and soon after, there was a shake-up at the Film Society, and the Festival's co-founder, Richard Roud, left the organization. I was there, and I think they needed somebody to replace Roud, so they said, "Well, now it's yours!" So that's how I got in.

What is your background? Was it film-related?

When I went to college, it was long enough ago that there wasn't really that much serious film study going on — just a handful of schools, but not very many. The place where I went to school had one film professor who had a big impact on me, and he inspired me to really seek a career in the field. So I started out being an academic and teaching film. I was on the verge of going to graduate school for an advanced degree, when I landed a job at the Art Institute of Chicago.

How many festivals do you get to a year now?

I really only go to two: Cannes and Berlin. However, I do attend other events as they fit into my schedule.

What is your favorite festival? What aspects of the event do you like and wish you could implement at NYFF?

Different festivals do different things so well. It just depends on what you're looking for, and whether or not the festival can satisfy that need.

Can you describe the process to submit to NYFF, and the selection process you have in place? Do you do any curating? Do you do any inviting?

Films come to us in a variety of ways. The majority just come in over the transom as we say. Some of them come in because they're by filmmakers whose work I know or whatever and I say "please submit your film." Other times people from various sorts of film promotion agencies that are out there send films — for example, something like the Austrian Film Commission will send you what they think are the three best films they have. Sometimes filmmakers who have already been in the Festival will contact me and say, "you and your team should really see this film," so yeah, with every film it's a little bit of a different story.

The submission process is pretty much open — anyone can send us a film. We don't have a submission fee. Because of that, we receive a lot of submissions from filmmakers all over the world.

Then we start looking at the films. I try to get through as many as I can, and my colleagues help out as well. Last year, we received over 2,000 submissions that we whittled down to probably around 100 by the middle of July.

At that point, four others and myself who are on the selection committee, start the process of talking and arguing. After our views are presented, about another 30 to 40 drop out, so we are down to a manageable 60. That's truly when it gets very tough! Of course, we're only going to take about half that number, but you re-watch, and re-argue, and ultimately, have to decide which of the ones you can take.

So of the 5 screeners, do you guys watch the films in their entirety?

I'm the one who watches most of the films, and I don't watch them in their entirety. We're a small festival showing only 25-28 films a year. For whatever reason, after about 15-20 minutes, it's clear to me that a film does not get a day in the ballpark — or even in the top 100 or 150 films, so there's really no reason for me to keep watching. I have to get on to the next one. Watching 2,000 films requires a lot of time.

I might watch something and think it's pleasant or enjoyable and nicely made, but it's just not going to make that final cut. I just have to arbitrarily make a decision. Having been at this post for many years, I have some sense of the types of films that will play.

If I see a film that I believe could be a good addition to another one of our programs, such as the Human Rights Watch Film Festival or our Latin Beat program or the New York Jewish Film Festival, I'll recommend the film to those events.

Do you give feedback to any of the filmmakers regarding your decisions?

I try not to. There are just too many films, and I don't really remember them well enough to give valuable feedback. You know, I take some notes for myself, but they aren't really for publication or sharing. Beyond that, if it's a film by a friend or somebody I know well, and he or she asks me why it didn't get in, I'll try and give them some information, because on a personal, as well as a professional level, I have to explain our decision. But if someone calls me out of the blue and says, "I would like to have the comments," — we just don't do that.

Do you find media kits or cover letters important when you're making decisions?

No. I really don't. I think they're just useful because if you select a film then you have all that material at your disposal if you need it — and it helps to not have to track down the filmmaker. But it has no influence whatsoever on our decision.

What are some of the biggest mistakes filmmakers make when submitting their films?

It's hard to really say. I think sometimes people send letters and they include a recommendation from somebody. I think that's kind of an odd strategy, and it never works for me. Maybe it works for other people, but I'm not sure it does.

Just present your film in the most dignified form. If there are aspects or information that you feel would be helpful for the selectors, let us know. Sometimes, especially toward the end of the process, we receive films that are not in their final form. In that case it helps if you can send a note about what the final form of the film will be.

Do you guys watch online screeners?

I don't know how long we'll be able to resist them, but I really don't find it to be a very conducive way of making a serious judgment about a film. I ask filmmakers to please send us a DVD — and most people do.

Does NYFF offer jury prizes?

No prizes whatsoever.

Does the Festival offer filmmakers travel or food or lodging?

We do for every film that's in the Festival. We offer a set amount for the director to do whatever they want with it. If the film is coming from a country that will pay the way for filmmakers to travel to New York, or a filmmaker stays with family or friends in the city, then it's a bit easier for us to say, "Here, take this lump sum do what you want with it."

How much is it? Is the sum the same for everyone or is it different?

I'd rather not tell you, as the amount changes every year based on funding, but it's the same for everybody.

With so many festivals out there, how can a filmmaker tell a good one from a bad one?

Well, I think what you have to ask is not "what you can do for the film festival," but "what the film festival can do for you"? I mean, you have to think, "What am I going to get out of this? Why would I send my film somewhere to people I don't know with circumstances I'm unaware of?" Wherever you send your film should do some good for you as well as the film. Generally speaking, one should be very defensive and figure out, "Okay, I want my film to go to this festival or that. If I can't get it there, then the next level down is..." and take it from there.

I think filmmakers also spend too much time on the festival road. Some filmmakers are still traveling with their firm a year and a half after the film first screened. That's fine if you're only interested in having a good time, but after a while they really should just end the quest.

What are your thoughts about premiere status?

That's one of the advantages about having a small festival — I can't really get worried about that. First of all, I think it's only really a concern to the film's producer, more so than to the film director. All of the films we show are New York premieres, and the vast majority of them are U.S. premieres, but we don't require it. A number of the films shown in our festival screened at Telluride or Toronto.

Our festival is for the New York public. And very few New Yorkers go to those festivals — a few hundred, tops. For us, the important thing is that *we* selected it and *we* are showing it. So we try to focus on that.

When you're making decisions and watching films, are you influenced at all by the accolades a film won somewhere else?

You know, being human I can't really say I'm not. Obviously, if I hear, "Oh they loved it in Venice," or "It was the best film," — yeah, that sticks in your mind. But in the end, you have to go with your own reaction. I mean, I'm not presenting a film festival as a subset of Venice — I'm presenting the NYFF, so we have to find something that we believe in. Sometimes our tastes match up with our colleagues, and very often they don't. So, it doesn't really matter.

Do you often feel pressure to take big names in films? Are you ever persuaded by distributors to take a film?

There's really no way anyone can pressure us. I mean, they can threaten us or call us names, but really, there's nothing they can do. I'd have to say that my board of directors protects my staff, the other selectors, and me from that kind of pressure. In the end, if you don't really believe in the film it's not worth it.

How important is your audience in your final selection process?

New York City has 7 or 8-odd million people, so what is our audience? You can find an audience for anything, when you get down to it. So, in that sense, you could say the audience is important because we love our houses to be full, and we love to have lots of people watching movies. I think all of us are dedicated to selecting and presenting films that need to be seen and appreciated by large numbers of people. But you can't force that. You just hope you select the work that can go beyond the confines of the Festival.

Have you ever programmed a film that you loved, but the audience just didn't get?

Sure. Listen, sometimes, there are films that really appeal to my colleagues or me, and then we show it at the Festival, and people just don't get it. Maybe they don't see what's interesting. Sometimes a bad review has a snowball effect. I mean, afterwards, I might watch the film again to see if I still feel the same way — and the majority of times, I do. I feel like we made the right decision, and even though people abhorred a film, we didn't. It's just as simple as that. We're known as a festival that makes choices: "yes" to some films and "no" to many more. And I think that's part of our reputation — and that's a good thing.

You touched on this, but are programming decisions ever dictated by sponsors or donors?

No. When people sign on to sponsor the NYFF, they have a pretty good idea of what we're up to, and if they didn't like what we were up to, they wouldn't come our way. With most sponsors, we've had a very cordial relationship, and I think we give them something that they can be proud of.

When you put your schedule together, do you program thematically, or by the audience, or by other factors?

I wish we had the liberty to program films any way we want, but we simply don't. Nowadays, with so many festivals in the world, filmmakers will tell us,

"Oh I'm so glad to show at NYFF, but I can only be there the first weekend." And since we want to have as many filmmakers as possible in attendance, they already made the decision for us.

Other times, we have a little more control. There are films you want to show on a Friday or Saturday night because those are big nights when people go out. So, yeah, we do little things like that. But, again, very often people dictate the program to us because of the circumstances of their lives.

Do you ever have to cut a film because it doesn't fit into your final schedule?

Never. We keep a careful eye out to see how many slots we've got left, and then you know, invite accordingly.

Are your decisions ever affected by the programming at other festivals in New York?

No. I mean the only thing we really require is that the film be a New York premiere. So we don't really look at the programming of other festivals in the area. They do their own thing, and we do ours.

What elements do you think add up to make a successful movie?

Selecting films is an enormously arbitrary process. For me, there's some kind of great continuum where on one side is astonishing, formal innovation, and on the other side is remarkable social relevance. The best films meet somewhere in the middle. Some films go more in one direction, and some go the other, but films that are both interesting as works of art, and have something to say, are the films that mean the most to me.

Are there any taboos — subject matter you just won't touch?

No.

Are there any recent thematic trends that have been overused?

No. Certainly, if you spend the summer, as I do, going through 600-700 American independent films, after a while, you really don't care if someone's just broken up with their girlfriend — because that's the subject of about 85 percent of them. But then all of a sudden, you'll see a film that has that plot and is good! You can't really judge that way. But I know a certain amount of weariness forms after awhile.

There is often a collective mind-set. When we look at the films we've invited for the Festival, sometimes, there is a sense that, "Hmm, we sure have a lot of films about child abuse" or, "We have a lot of films about divorced couples." And you don't know what that's from — maybe it's just something in the air that we've somehow latched onto. Every now and then you feel, "Hey, there's a real movement for this kind of film."

What do you think is more important: schooling or storytelling?

I think school has been phenomenally important for a number of filmmakers that I know, and I think other people who didn't go to a film school are doing perfectly well. So, it's a very personal thing. I don't think there's a formula. It depends on where you are, and your stage of life, and what school can offer you. I don't think there's anything cut-and-dry about it, it's kind of case by case.

What web sites and publications do you regularly read?

I don't read very many, unfortunately — I don't have that much time. So, I try every now and then to catch up with what my friend Dave Kehr is saying on his website, or David Bordwell or Jonathan Rosenbaum. But let's just say, I'm a pretty infrequent visitor to those sites. I just don't have time.

I tend to actually read the print version of *Variety* when it comes in the office, and obviously I read *The New York Times*. I read a couple of other critics whose work I like and keep up with, and try and keep up with some foreign journalists whose work I like, but I can't really trawl the blogs too much.

Do you have a favorite success story? Maybe a film that played NYFF and ended up doing really well, or perhaps someone you coached?

I think it's more film and filmmakers. For example, a pair of filmmakers we've been very close to for a long time are the Dardenne Brothers. We showed their film *La Promesse* in 1995, and pretty much have shown almost all their works. We've done retrospectives of their work, and I think they are extraordinary artists and wonderful people. And this year at the NYFF, when our colleague, Scott Foundas introduced them on the stage, the entire audience leapt to its feet and gave them a standing ovation. It was incredibly moving for all of us. They are artists who really came from nowhere, and within 15 years, I think, for this audience, they've established themselves as artists of the first rank. Even though their films do not have commercial successes in the US, there is a group of people in New York who truly know and appreciate the nature of their art.

What's the nicest thing or compliment that a filmmaker's ever said to you?

I'm very proud of our presentation. I think one of the things that we really emphasize at Lincoln Center is that presentation is every bit as important as selection. So you have to really make sure the films are presented properly, and in all the best ways.

I remember years ago, we had the great Spanish filmmaker, Víctor Erice, for a retrospective of his work. We were supposed to go out to dinner after he introduced his film, *Dream of Light* (aka *Quince Tree of the Sun*). He started watching some of the film — you know filmmakers do to make sure everything is in focus — and when I mentioned we should probably leave, he said, "Do you mind if we went out to dinner later? It's just such a pleasure to watch my film in your theater. I'd really prefer to sit and watch." That really was very moving to me because Victor is someone who is an incredible cinephile, and for him to say it looked and sounded so perfect — that is the ultimate compliment. It really meant a lot to me, because I don't think he was the type of man to just say it — he really meant it.

Would you share one of the worst things a filmmaker's ever said to you?

There was one time when we had John Boorman come to screen *Point Blank*. We were doing a test screening when a projectionist, who no longer works with us, was showing the film in scope, and out of sheer laziness, did not mask the screen properly. Boorman was absolutely furious that the film was not masked properly, and really ran us over the coals in the press conference. He later calmed down, and at the public screening, he was very happy with the proper projection.

Do you have a secret blacklist?

I couldn't possibly afford that. I sort of have to keep myself open for the best work. I mean, there are filmmakers I don't particularly like as people, but they are quite talented. All I can ask of anyone is to come and behave civilly. They don't have to be my pals — in fact, very few of them are.

How do you see the impact of changing technologies on the quality of films you're seeing recently?

It's always a double-edged sword. I think the digital technology has obviously created much greater access to great range of filmmakers. So you have, from all over, people making films, which is great. Groups that were formerly underrepresented, now have the ability to make film. This is probably the greatest contribution digital filmmaking has given us.

On the other hand, there are concerns about digital shooting. For example, the fact that you can just keep shooting without fear of running out of film, I think sometimes ruins or lessens the concept of actually creating a shot — the idea of framing and composition and knowing exactly what you want to shoot. Shoot all you want, and the cost is the same, and there is an hour on your tape instead of ten minutes on a reel.
I also think that, for a while, when people started doing online editing, there was a tendency to overload a film with special effects. I think after a while, filmmakers calmed down and stopped using them just because they could, and now use them in a way that I find a little more agreeable.

In the end, do you think digital filmmaking is a positive, negative, or neutral?

Sometimes I say, "The great thing about digital is that we receive so many films, and the bad thing about digital is that we receive so many films."

I mean, you receive an enormous amount of films, because now people can not only make films, but send them to you in digital formats at a fraction of what it cost to send a 35mm print around. But on the other hand, although it means more work, it means more access to more titles.

Of the people I'm interviewing, you've been in film the longest. How do you keep your passion?

Well, of course it's a new job every year. Yes, in a way, certain aspects of the job remain the same, but on the whole, the job itself changes because the films change.

I think every year, we look at the Festival and criticize it and come up with ways to improve it over the previous year. Last year, for the first time, we had access to the new Elinor Bunim Monroe Film Center, which had just opened in June. The additional venue allowed us to do a lot of sidebar and complimentary programming. I think we were nervous going into that, but frankly, in my opinion it worked splendidly. I think it gave the Festival more character, and audiences really enjoyed those films. We look forward to doing that again — and strive to do it even better.

If you could give would-be entrants one piece of advice, what would it be?

Send us the work that you think best represents your film. Something I don't like is when a filmmaker — especially an unknown filmmaker — says, "I rushed so hard to get this to you. I know that your deadline is in three days." Don't rush your work — *Do* your work. And if you don't get into the NYFF, maybe you'll get into Sundance, or maybe you'll get to direct some other films, or maybe you'll get into who knows what? But don't rush for a festival. Make your film. You spend so much time and money — why would you rush to meet my deadline? That should be the least of your worries. So, make your film. If your film comes in on time so that we can judge it and everything works out — fabulous. But if not, there are a lot of other festivals out there. And we will still be here next year.

What three words best describe what you do?

I think I'm in the film history business. As a film curator and festival director, I try and point out the most significant films from both the present and the past, and help give a sense of shape and actually a kind of narrative to film history.

"FASCINATING. MULTIDIMENSIONAL. DEMANDING." SUSAN BAROCAS

Former Director, Washington Jewish Film Festival

About the Festival:

- Founded in 1990, the Washington Jewish Film Festival aims to show the diversity of the Jewish experience — cultural, religious, interpersonal, historical — as well as the universality of it and to bring people together over these kinds of shared universal themes.
- 11-day event for general audiences, targeting Jewish filmgoers and lovers of independent international cinema
- Website: wjff.org

Susan Barocas is director of the Washington Jewish Film Festival and the WJFF Year-Round program at the Washington, D.C. Jewish Community Center. Also a writer and filmmaker, her screen credits include *Jewish Cooking in America with Joan Nathan, Nightmare's End: The Liberation of the Camps* and *Coal Country.*

Susan and I have worked together on past projects in the D.C. area, and she has spoken numerous times at the annual Regional Film Festival Conference I coordinate for Mid-Atlantic festivals. She is a frequent traveler to festivals wide and far — so catching up for this interview was both a treat and a homecoming for the two of us.

What is the history of the Washington Jewish Film Festival?

The Festival was founded by a local filmmaker, Aviva Kempner, after she attended the San Francisco Jewish Film Festival — the first Jewish film festival in the country. She came to the DCJCC with the idea. Together with a handful of others, they created the first event at the old Biograph Theater in Georgetown with eight films. It has grown ever since. I am the third director, having started in 2008.

What is your background?

I spent 20+ years in non-profit public relations, during which time I worked on commercials, training films, video news releases, and PSAs for radio and television. I have always been interested in film, film festivals, and making documentary films. When I moved to D.C. from New York in 1993, I wanted to get involved in the community and the local film scene, so I volunteered for the WJFF and co-chaired the Public Relations Committee that first year. Through the years, I worked in various volunteer roles and also had a work-in-progress in the Festival in 2006. So the only thing left for me to do was to direct the Festival. At the time I was running my own PR/strategic communications company, and was also writing, producing, and directing freelance video and film projects. I have found that all of my prior experience and skills in films, public relations, public speaking and producing events all served me very well as a festival director.

Before becoming the director, did you attend other film festivals?

Yes. I was living in Denver in the late 1970s when the Denver International Film Festival first started — so I went. It was my first film festival and I got hooked. Later, when I lived in New York City, I would attend various film festivals and events there, and often volunteer.

Shortly after I moved to DC in 1993, I remember sitting in the audience at FilmFest DC when director Lina Wertmüller was speaking, and I realized — I want to make films and I want to bring films to audiences. There was something that appealed to me so much. For me now to head WJFF and also volunteer as the FilmFest DC Circle Award jury chair is so exciting for me, and very fulfilling.

Which film festivals do you currently attend?

I go to the Berlin and Jerusalem film festivals every year. Last year, I also went to the Jewish Film Festival in San Francisco (the mother of all Jewish film festivals) and New York and then other film festivals around the area to see how they operate and to network.

Do you have a favorite festival? What part of that event would you like to take from it?

So far, my overall favorite is the Berlinale. The atmosphere in all the parts of the city where the Festival takes place is all about film and filmmakers. People are sitting outside in the middle of winter in cafes discussing films. Throughout the Festival, I love going from theater to theater, seeing film after film from all over the world as well as the accessibility to the filmmakers in theaters, at the market and in lobbies, cafes, on lines waiting for films. In addition, the market in Berlin is quite large, second only to the market at Cannes, which gives me terrific access to finding films it would otherwise be difficult to unearth, and to developing good working relationships with distributors, country film commissions, production companies and, of course, the filmmakers themselves.

As a presenter, I love the connection between the audience and the filmmaker. I hope to promote the same feeling that I get at other good festivals I attend, like Berlin, where the guest filmmakers are very much a part of the festival and accessible to the audience. It is very special to see what a difference it makes to the audience to have the filmmakers present. And for the filmmakers, they get the direct response of the audience — when they laugh or cry or collectively hold their breath. I also have realized that people are hungry to learn about film and truly appreciate the opportunity to get to know about other people, other worlds, outside their own. Film is a bridge, a connection. I love that. It is very special, and can help change the world in its own special ways, even if just a little bit at a time.

Can you describe the submission process at WJFF?

The WJFF is professionally curated, meaning I have the final word when it comes to the programming. We don't have a formal screening committee, so you can imagine that I see a lot of films each year, usually somewhere around 300. Every film that comes in is recorded and tracked on our master spread sheet that includes each new film as well as what we have already in inventory from other years, but have not shown for whatever reason.

I have discovered that for the unsolicited submissions — those that come over the website or are just mailed to the office — I don't have the time to watch all of them, so I have developed a small, select group of people, nearly all of whom have experience professionally in film/video and who are active volunteers with the WJFF, and they do some pre-screening for the Festival. We have a form, and the reviewers must write up a short synopsis of the film and if they recommend a yes, no, or maybe, and why. If they give it a "yes" or "maybe" rating, I will always watch it. If they say give it a "no" rating, I'll have a conversation with that person to find out why: Is it a poorly told story? Is it not a fit for our audience? Are the production values so poor that it detracts from the film too much? If I am on the fence or if the reviewer is on the fence, I might pass it to someone else before it gets to me. Truth is that I see at least some of nearly every film anyway — I love to watch films!

It is important that I don't program just for my tastes when I select films. I select for a wide audience. People always ask if I like a certain film. For me, that is only part of the question. Does the film have value? Will the audience relate to it? Should the film be included, perhaps in a smaller venue, if only 30 attend the screening, but it has something special — and by showing it, I encourage the filmmaker? Also, what themes have come to the surface across several films? And I have to consider the balance of the whole festival program, meaning genre, subject matter, age appeal, countries of production, and so on. There are so many factors! In the end, the selections get narrowed down to an A-list of definite choices and a B-list of possibles. I then go from there to program and juggle the schedule.

Did you create this system? Was it different before you got here?

Yes. And yes. The WJFF has always been professionally curated. But everybody has their own way to get the end result. Since I came on as director, the Festival has grown bigger than it ever was, so tracking the films in an orderly way has become more and more important. It also helps me program for our year-round films since I show 3-6 films every month.

What qualities make for a good film screener? Other than being your trusted friends?

Believe it or not, that's not a requirement at all! A good screener should be open-minded, look at how the film is made, how it is presented, what it is really about. There are topics that you might not like, but you must be open to viewing and understanding these films. You also have to be able to overlook your subjectivity — sometimes to be able to say that, while you do not like the film, it is an important film and there is an audience for it. You have to find if there is something about a film that compels you to watch it — whether it makes you laugh, cry, sit on the edge of your seat, or relax into it. You must select films that most people in the audience are glad they saw, even if it pisses them off. A good committee member should see — and be able to articulate that.

How long is your selection process?

All year. Along with the new films that constantly arrive, we track films submitted from other years and look at them again for the current year. I look for themes to present themselves. For example, last year, after looking at all the films, I had an incredible number by female directors from all over the world, 16 of whom I included in the Festival around a theme "Jewish Film/

Women Filmmakers." It turned out great!

What is your thought on online screeners?

We use them because we have to. Sometimes, that is the only way I can see some films. I don't like it, particularly the time constraints for access, but the truth is that I watch most on DVD on my computer or TV anyway. It would be better to watch in a theater, but we don't have those types of facilities.

Have you had problems with online screeners?

Yes, such as access codes that don't work or have expired. Also, if I can't read the subtitles on my computer screen, they usually won't be readable in a theater. Sometimes there are problems with the compression and the image is warped or distorted. If it is the only way I can see a film, then so be it.

Do you give feedback to filmmakers about the selection process?

Not as a matter of course or as much as I would like to. One reason is that I am the only staff person most of the year, and am programming another 3-6 films each month, so I just don't have time. However, if someone emails me, I will give them feedback as much as possible.

Do you find media kits helpful?

Not in making selections, but they are very important after the selection process is complete. They should have photos, a good synopsis, director's statement, reviews, cast...the usual. For the submission process, we do need a short synopsis with basic production details like country(s), year, language, length, director, formats available. Plus it's helpful to have maybe a page or two with the director's statement and additional background information, particularly if it sets the film apart or puts it in context I wouldn't otherwise know. Also important is contact information for follow up. You would be surprised how many people forget that very rather significant detail. Any additional information I need during the selection process I can usually find online or I will contact the filmmaker or distributor.

What is the biggest mistake a filmmaker can make when submitting to your festival?

Being arrogant. I don't want to be told, "What do you mean you are not accepting my film for your festival?" or, "I don't really need to send you a screener. You can just call up so and so. They showed it." One of the best things someone can do is submit on time with complete information.

Do you have a secret blacklist?

I don't have a blacklist. I do have filmmakers that I think are less enjoyable to work with than others, but some of them produce really good work, so I must figure out how to work with them. It's not personal. It's about what is on the screen.

There have been many programming situations where I have had too many good films — all of equal value — and I needed to eliminate some. In that case, I might consider the filmmaker as a possible guest, and then how difficult they are to work with comes into play. If we incur the effort and expense of bringing a filmmaker here, I want the best possible prospects that the audience will have a good relationship with the filmmaker and get a lot out of him/her being here. Sadly, it has happened in the past that a few difficult filmmakers have made things really unenjoyable for me and even occasionally for the audience. The good news is that doesn't happen 99 percent of the time.

Does WJFF pay screening fees?

Yes we do. We have to most of the time. This is a conflict for me because as a festival director, I am always trying to get the best deal possible and many international film festivals do not pay screening fees. It seems my budget is always running over because the fees keep increasing! But as a filmmaker, I know it is hard, expensive work to make a film, and I would like to be fairly compensated for my work and want to do the same for all the filmmakers in my festival.

I do respect paying screening fees, but what I don't respect is that some fees have gotten totally out of hand. Some distributors have outrageous screening fees. There was one distributor whose films I did not show for two years because I could not afford his fees. If I had shown two of his films, I would have had to eliminate several other films. There is a balance of what you can do and what you have to do.

Are you under a lot of pressure from film distributors?

Over the years, I have learned that sometimes a distributor will say that a film is "perfect" for my festival, but it turns out to be their "flavor of the month."

It is up to me as the festival director to make programming decisions based on what is best for my festival and my audiences. I appreciate distributors who really get to know the Festival and recommend films that are appropriate and appealing for us.

There have also been times when there has been a misunderstanding between my interest in a film and my commitment to program it. I have learned to be very, very clear in my dealings with distributors and filmmakers, and I commit more to writing quick emails to confirm conversations so my intent is, hopefully, very apparent.

I also really appreciate distributors who are willing to negotiate screening fees or occasionally who give us films as in-kind contributions, for which I will list them as I would any other sponsor who donates or knocks a significant amount like $1,000 or $2,000 off the price of something we would be purchasing.

What are your thoughts on premiere status?

Sometimes I think it is probably more important to me than anyone in the audience! For the media, it does help when you tell them we have four world-premieres and three US-premieres in one festival — they pick up on that. Donors also pick up on it, because there is a certain prestige level with which they want to be associated. Last year, we showed the US premiere of a film on opening night, and now that the film is making the rounds in theaters. Our audience has been emailing me about how cool it is that they were there first.

Are you influenced by accolades a film might have received at other festivals or events?

Only if I am on the fence about my decision of whether or not to program a film. Sometimes I look at what other people said and ask myself, "What am I missing?" For example, I showed a film in the 2011 WJFF that was a Sundance winner and has been winning awards all over. I still have some reservations about the film, yet we ended up selling out the screenings because of the buzz. I might not have programmed it if I wasn't nudged in that direction by the accolades. What I find really interesting is that the audience reaction was split, like mine.

Are you influenced by big names in films?

We have shown some big films with big names, and it's nice for prestige as well as our box office. For example, we were the first in the US to show *The Debt* with Helen Mirren. The deal was we couldn't say it was a premiere, so we listed as a "sneak peek" and sold out the program in a few days. You better believe I used Helen Mirren's picture on the cover of the program that year! What I really care about are compelling characters in well told stories that "come off the screen" to me — whether it's a feature film or documentary. So there are some films with big names I have chosen not to show because, bottom line, I didn't believe they met the criteria.

Would you pick a big-name film over a no-name one?

Not necessarily. It's always the question of finding balance. All things being equal, I probably would try to find a slot for both of them. I am lucky that I have the luxury of programming year-round as well as the Festival, so I can show films I can't fit into the Festival programming. That way the audience still gets to see it.

How important is your audience in making selection decisions?

My audience is very important. I'm always thinking about the audience, not just what I think is an easy sell (although we always need some of those!), but my goal is also to educate the audience, to push them a bit, to open their eyes, hearts and minds to new ideas and perspectives. I program because I think an audience should see something.

Have you ever programmed a film you loved and the audience did not?

Oh, yes. I can think of a few, and they shall remain nameless. I remember one in particular that had 18 people in a 200-seat theater. I was so disappointed, and I still think that it's an outstanding, worthwhile film! It was a documentary, very personal but with overriding universal themes. It seems documentaries, which I love and also make, can be a harder sell to the audience than features or even shorts.

Did you feel it had to be shown or were you surprised by the audience attendance?

Both! I was surprised, as was our festival coordinator at the time, who also loved the film. It was very worth seeing and I'm not sure where the "miss" came in, which does sometimes happen and can keep me up at night if I let it!

What role do donors or sponsors play in your selection process?

I am lucky — donors play almost no role in my actual selection process. That being said, after the films are selected, I do coordinate the schedule as much as possible so my daily sponsors have films they are particularly drawn to screening on their sponsored day. That gives donors a stake in the process and encourages them to bring their guests to the Festival for "their" films.

I am delighted when I can program a film that matches a donor or sponsor's goals. In 2010, for example, we had a potential sponsor who had a special interest in supporting people with disabilities. Because I wanted to program an outstanding film that matched their interest, that donor became the sponsor of the day that film was shown. But it didn't work the other way around — the film drove the selection process, not the donor.

Also, we work with many embassies and cultural organizations to show films from 14-20 countries a year. They are wonderful partners by supporting us financially, helping us get films, providing venues and bringing in filmmakers. A good example was when Argentina had its Bicentennial in 2010, and I worked with the embassy because Argentinean Jewish film is very significant in the world of Jewish cinema. It was an excellent, mutually beneficial connection that enabled us to show more Argentinean films and to bring leading Argentinean filmmaker Daniel Berman to the WJFF to accept our annual Visionary Award.

I know you curate films from other festivals. Do you consult with other festival programmers first?

It is a very enriching part of my job to have that special relationship with other festival directors. In fact, if you look at our programs, we often thank each other. One of the highlights of the Berlin Film Festival every year is the special dinner with all the Jewish Film Festival directors and programmers. We exchange catalogs and talk about films, what happened over the past year and what we see coming up. We also talk about good guests — and the bad ones! Each of the festival directors I interact with throughout the year still maintains their own individual festival "personality," but working cooperatively always makes the end product better.

Are you influenced by other festival catalogs?

First, I love looking at other festival catalogs from a design point of view and that can spark ideas for me. Second, there is both a certain amount of ego involved and it also keeps me on my toes. I do look at catalogs and, honestly, I have a certain satisfaction in knowing that we showed the film first or we did extra programming around a film that made it even more special. Other catalogs are yet another good resource for films I haven't shown, sometimes including a film we could not get and it alerts me that it is now available.

Since we are one of the biggest Jewish film festivals around, I know others are looking at my catalog also. As soon as my program goes up online, I get a flurry of emails asking me for distributor information for various films. This continues throughout the year. I find that to be a nice compliment to our programming.

You are in a market that is saturated with film festivals (there are 85+ film festivals in the greater Washington, D.C. area). How does programming around these festivals affect what you are showing?

I work with many of the other area festivals all year long, whether DC Shorts, Film Neu (German), FilmFest DC, Reel Affirmations, or others. Since we are specifically a Jewish film festival, I like to be the one to show as many of the films that fit our niche as possible. I do talk about what we are showing or planning to show, and what their plans are, so we try to make sure we aren't stepping on each other's toes. But in the end, it is not about money or "ownership" — it's all about cooperating to bring films to audiences. So, I'll co-sponsor screenings at other festivals to help spread the word and expand the audience for films. It also exposes my festival to new audiences, so it's a win-win.

What is more important — schooling or storytelling?

I think storytelling is first and foremost. Without good storytelling, it is hard to engage an audience. And, after all, film really is all about telling stories.

What elements add up to make a successful film?

As I said, the story is primary and then comes how you tell it — character, clarity, emotion, the visual components, and so on. It is a delicate balance of all the elements. For me, the most successful films move me, make me feel something, and in some way open up a world to me that I have not yet seen or seen in that way.

What are some triggers or taboos that make you want to turn off a film?

First of all, I love films and have trouble turning off any film — unless it is really offensive to me or would be to the majority of my audience. I won't show excessive gore, or gratuitous violence or harm to children or animals. Although I show films about the Holocaust, and they can show extremely difficult scenes including violence and scenes that have been very difficult for me to sit through, there is a reason for showing these scenes and how they are shown makes a tremendous difference.

I admire when a filmmaker demonstrates violence without showing guts and gore. A good example of this is *Wunderkinder*, a film from our last festival in which a Nazi officer peels an apple while talking to a young girl. The subtext of the scene is intensely violent beyond almost anything I have recently seen. It is one of the most chilling scenes I have ever seen in any film — and my fifteen year-old son felt the same way. To me, that is brilliant filmmaking.

If I am fortunate enough to attend your festival, what should I do to get the best experience from it?

See everything. Okay, if that won't work, see films you might not ordinarily go see. Challenge yourself. See films you might not know anything about or don't think you want to know anything about. See a film from a country you don't know about, or see a mystery when you love musicals — stretch yourself.

Do you have a favorite success story?

We have had a few. *A Matter of Size* is an Israeli movie that played WJFF first, and then went on to a full commercial release. I feel I had a part in getting it shown commercially. Another is *The Gift to Stalin* from Kazakhstan. After playing in our festival, it played all over at many other festivals. It was a beautiful film and I am happy to know that we had a hand in that. It feels really good when that happens.

We have had filmmakers make amazing connections. They will come to the Festival and meet, and then in a year or two, they are making films together. And filmmakers find distributors at WJFF. For example, Michael Verhoffen, a German filmmaker, met the director of the National Center for Jewish Film here, and now she is his distributor and they became good friends as well.

What is the nicest thing a filmmaker has said to you?

I have been very fortunate. I have been told from numerous guests that WJFF is the best festival — and best organized festival — that they have ever attended, also that we have the best audiences. That feels really nice. People have even made donations to the Festival in my name. That is incredibly powerful and I am so grateful. But I think the absolutely best thing a guest ever said about me is that I am the "most committed and genuine person" he has worked with so far and that I really went out of my way to make his stay comfortable. Wow! That's a lot of gas in my tank!

What is the worst thing a filmmaker has ever said to you?

I once had an unpleasant situation with two filmmakers concerning extra expenses while they were here. We have certain policies that were clear to me, but apparently not to them. They told me I don't care about filmmakers at my festival, which stung. Fortunately, I know that's not true and needless to say, I am much clearer now when I book guests.

How do you schedule/program your festival — what is the process? Do you find that the way you program determines the slots for films?

It is a huge puzzle, and each year I am amazed that I can figure it out! There are so many elements. I create a master "A" list that has more films on it than I can possibly show. Once I have that list, I start to take into account all the other factors beginning with when the film is available during my festival dates and in what formats. Then I have to look at my 8-10 venues to determine which can show what formats and when. I have to consider the audience, as certain audiences "go with" certain venues and also certain times. I look at the possibilities of bringing in a guest and when is that person available.

Overall, there is an important balance of film subject matter and genres. I am not going to show 30 Holocaust films or too many Israeli films, although I think they are some of the best films we screen. A lot of them are documentaries, and we are not exclusively a doc festival, so I need to balance features vs. docs vs. shorts. I also like to show films from as many countries as possible because I think that adds to the flavor of the Festival.

And, of course, I have to think about what will probably sell best and make money vs. how many films I can show that might just break even or do less than that at the box office, but are important films to show anyway.

What are the thematic trends in the films coming across your desk now? Are any overused?

I see a trend of more women filmmakers producing better and better films — especially full-length features. That's why last year I had a special focus on women making films with Jewish content. We had 16 women directors represented in the Festival, 17 films out of 47. That's way better than Hollywood's average!

I am also seeing so many creative ways to tell Holocaust stories. This is important as we go forward telling the story of the Holocaust when there are no longer survivors. I am seeing more films about controversial events in the Holocaust, and also by or about children of perpetrators. I think some of the first-hand generation had to pass before many of these stories could be told. This is where filmmakers walk between family, myth, and history. A good example of this is a film we showed in 2010, *Two or Three Things I Know about Him*, which is such a powerful film. The director told the audience that while his mother was alive, he couldn't even discuss the topic of his father's role as the Ambassador to Slovakia during Hitler's regime. His father was an early friend of Hitler's and signed the papers deporting Slovakia's Jews, yet the rest of the filmmaker's family denies the father knew anything about what was going on.

Another overall trend is that documentaries are getting better and better, and finding bigger audiences, which is so satisfying both as a programmer and a doc filmmaker. I find the docs from Israel to be among the best in general — compelling, willing to tackle tough subjects, insightful, very well crafted with high production values.

Do you attribute this to film schools or technology?

Actually, I think both technology, which has made filmmaking more accessible even if not always adding to a film's level of excellence, and the fact that we are obsessed with looking at ourselves. We can't walk by the mirror without looking! These factors have led to more interest in docs whereas 15 or 20 years ago, they were not as well-known to the general public. Some non-fiction TV programming has helped broaden their appeal, as well as the incredible and long-standing works of documentarians such as the Maysles brothers, D.A. Pennebaker and Chris Hegedus, Barbara Kopple, DC's own Aviva Kempner, and many other talented and tenacious documentary filmmakers.

Do you think your job as a programmer has jaded the way you see films or do you think it has expanded your appreciation of films?

My job has definitely expanded my appreciation of films and my admiration for filmmakers. Beyond my role as a programmer, as a filmmaker I have come to appreciate the challenges and effort festival directors put into programming their film events.

My appreciation for film itself is nearly boundless. I love going to movies! People think I am crazy because after WJFF is over, I want to go see films in movie theaters that I've missed because I've been so busy with the Festival. There is something very special about sitting in the dark with people you don't know and sharing an experience for that certain time, an experience that each of us takes away into our own lives from that shared moment.

If you could give a would-be entrant one piece of advice, what would it be?

Above all, make a good film. Don't send something that is less than the best you can do. That being said, don't take rejection personally. Know that even if your film truly is a masterpiece, it might not fit a particular festival's perspective or fit into that year's balance of films. Keep doing good work and believing in your work!

As a festival director, I would also encourage filmmakers to research and develop a festival strategy. Don't send your film to every festival in the world. Have a plan. Target your submissions. You'll save money and aggravation, and in the end, your film will nearly always get the right exposure it deserves.

What three words best describe what you do?

1. Fascinating
2. Multidimensional
3. Demanding

"INSPIRE. EDUCATE. ENTERTAIN" SEATTLE INTERNATIONAL FILM FESTIVAL

Dustin Kaspar, Educational Programs Manager
Beth Barrett, Director of Programming

About the Festival:

- Founded in 1976, SIFF's mission is to create experiences that bring people together to discover extraordinary films from around the world. "It is through the art of cinema that we foster a community that is more informed, aware, and alive."
- 25-day event for general audiences; event targeting local film enthusiasts
- Website: siff.net

The Seattle International Film Festival (SIFF) is currently the largest film festival in the United States with more than 150,000 attendees in 2011. Two of the reasons for SIFF's amazing success are Dustin and Beth.

Before delving into the world of film festivals, Dustin Kaspar worked as a secondary choral music educator. A graduate of University of Illinois at Urbana-Champaign, Dustin wanted more out of arts education that he could share with others. It was his commitment to make a more substantial influence upon arts education and his affinity for cinema that brought Dustin to film festivals. Dustin has worked with five film festivals including Port Townsend Film Festival, Seattle Lesbian and Gay Film Festival and Olympia Film Festival. Dustin currently works as the Educational Programs Manager for the Seattle International Film Festival. Another endeavor for Dustin includes his own film festival, Kaspar's Kouch Film Festival, currently in its second year of bi-weekly themed double features.

Beth has been with SIFF since 2003, and is currently responsible for managing all aspects of film programming, the staff of film programmers, and securing films and guests for the 25-day Festival. She is also instrumental in the programming and management of SIFF Cinema at the Film Center and the Uptown, as well as SIFF's other year-round programs. An aficionado of short films, she secured SIFF's status as an Academy Award qualifying festival in 2008. Beth has been in Seattle for 18 years and holds an MA in Northern Renaissance Art History.

What's the history of SIFF? How did it come to be almost four decades ago?

DUSTIN: Two Canadians came down from Vancouver to start a festival in the old historic Moore Theater here in Seattle. They ended up curating 18 films in 14 days back in 1976. And it grew considerably from there. Surprisingly, the Festival used to have a specific spotlight on Dutch film, for sometime. I don't know how long that lasted, but I do know that about its early past.

Is there a big Dutch community in Seattle?

BETH: Strangely enough, no. The two Canadians were Dan Ireland, who went on to direct *Whole Wide World, Mrs. Palfrey at the Claremont* and most recently *Jolene*, and Darryl Macdonald, who is now the executive director down at the Palm Springs International Film Festival. Those two guys came across the border and started the Festival. And they just loved Dutch film, and for a little while, were the Dutch film distributors for the U.S.

DUSTIN: And I'm just going to add, in 1979 SIFF had the world premiere of Alien, and got a big boost from that in terms of awareness of the Festival. Since then, we have screened the world premieres of *Empire Strikes Back* and *Return of the Jedi* — we happened to be at the right time of year for these types of films.

How did you become involved in the Festival?

BETH: I have actually no film background. I failed my very first film mid-term, "History of Film 101." But I went on to get an MA in art history. I became involved in the lesbian and gay film festival here in Seattle, and attended SIFF as a ticket holder every year. It was a great way to make friends. Then I moved to Sydney, and worked with the Mardi Gras Film Festival and then the Sydney Film Festival. When I came back to the States, I had decided that I really wanted to work in festivals.

DUSTIN: I've been a film lover for most of my early life. I never went to a film festival until I was 22, and didn't really realize what it was I was missing. I fell whole heartedly in love with it, and became a pass holder for three years, insatiably consuming as much as possible in 25 days. At the time, I was a full-time choir teacher, and loved arts education. When attending SIFF, I realized that film festivals are an education, and what we choose to show and what we choose to program affects the community. I ended up volunteering and I got my foot in my door.

So, how long have each of you been with SIFF?

BETH: This will be my tenth festival.

DUSTIN: Let's see, my first was '06, so this will be my seventh festival in 2012.

BETH: Wow, long time.

DUSTIN: Yeah, don't remind me.

Ha ha! So, other than SIFF, how many other or what other festivals do you go to now?

DUSTIN: I've been going to Toronto for the past couple of years, been around to Berlin, Clermont-Ferrand Short Film Festival, as well as regional festivals – Vancouver, Port Townsend and Portland.

BETH: And this year, Toronto, Vancouver, and I'm actually in the middle of booking all the inter-continental travel...I'm going to Rotterdam, Gothenburg and Berlin.

What are parts of other festivals you admire and wish you could bring back to SIFF?

BETH: The thing I love about Berlin is the pure crush of films, because with the market right there, you can see about eight or nine films a day — which is amazing! I really love Vancouver because it's audience-focused, and our audiences are very similar. In fact, a lot of our pass holders are pass holders at Vancouver. They operate primarily within a 7-plex, so you're surrounded by the same people seeing the same films. I sit and talk to pass holders, and that's my way of getting that kind of wonderful community experience. I love that camaraderie.

DUSTIN: I think one of the things that I like most about going to festivals is the ability to see as much as possible. I love interacting with the people who are making movies and having that opportunity to dig deeper into the art form. The Port Townsend Film Festival shows not only fabulous movies, but finds new ways for filmmakers to engage with the public.

Can you describe, in detail, the submission process and the selection process at SIFF? It must be quite an undertaking with almost 5,000 films to review.

BETH: So, a filmmaker can submit one of two ways – through Withoutabox, or a paper entry form. They send us their DVD and it gets logged into our database. We have a system where all films are rated from one to nine. All films start off at an eight until we review them. Each film is watched by at least one programmer, or two to four pre-screening committee members, who we need to watch many of the feature-length submissions. We will use their aggregate grades to move the film up or down the scale to indicate whether a programmer should watch it, or three additional pre-screeners. Every film is watched in its entirety by at least one member of the programming team.

In their entirety? Everything?

DUSTIN: 5,000 submissions — that's a lot.

BETH: We have a lot of pre-screeners.

Well, how many pre-screeners do you have?

BETH: Right now we have seventeen.

DUSTIN: And the programming committee as well, there's fifteen of us?

BETH: We're also watching all the submissions. We try to send some of the blind submissions through the pre-screening committee. With the advent of digital technology, anyone can make a film. That means that *anyone* can make a film. Our programming team has a limited number of eyeball hours, so we like to not weed out, but pre-select.

DUSTIN: I think I watched 500 to 600 features last year. Easily.

How long do you have to watch all of these films?

BETH: We start the submission process at the beginning of August and end in January. We generally announce the films in May, so we have about nine months to review and program.

How many of your pre-screeners or screening committee members are film professionals?

DUSTIN: Probably a third of them are film professionals, and the rest of us are film lovers. It's a pretty good mix.

Like most festivals, you guys charge a submission fee. But with a budget of almost

$6M, why do you charge the fee?

BETH: To support the programmers — we pay our programmers with the film submission fees. I actually think that submission fees self-select films. People who just throw a film together and are unsure of whether it's a good movie or a bad movie will most likely not spend money to enter. Which is not a bad thing, because the film is probably not something we would program.

Do you offer fee waivers?

BETH: We have certain organizations, film organizations, mostly European, that we have been working with years, who will send us a selection of the newest films. They, festival alumni, and films that were produced in the state of Washington, share the majority of our fee waivers.

What are your thoughts about online screeners?

DUSTIN: You know, I'm actually coming around to it because I don't like needless shipping costs. I'm not sure I feel that the technology is 100 percent up to speed yet, both in terms of quality, and of every programmer having a computer that can play the files without stopping every twenty seconds.

BETH: It also allows filmmakers from countries in Africa and South America to send us screeners in a reliable and inexpensive way. They don't have that financial barrier of $60 to send a DVD, or have to rely on a slow postal system.

Do you give feedback to filmmakers about their entries?

BETH: No, not as a matter of course. Occasionally, if the filmmaker asks really nicely, and not during the Festival, we will take some time to discuss. Otherwise we really don't have the time.

DUSTIN: The big challenge of that is (1) you want to have feedback to give, which is not always easy when we have a simple number scale, and (2) with 3,000 films submitted, it's tough to go through and give feedback while we're in the process of reviewing. It would take even more time to go back and try to re-watch a film so that you can give feedback after the fact. I know we've talked about giving feedback to local filmmakers, but we have not yet figured out a way to do it in a meaningful way.

Do you find media kits helpful in your decision-making process?

BETH: I would rather not receive them until we're done reviewing for the Festival, because they all end up in the recycle bin. I want to judge the film on the film itself, not on what a release or a publicist says.

What's the biggest mistake a filmmaker can make when submitting to a festival?

BETH: Repeatedly emailing the programming team — or worse, blanket emailing the entire department or staff of the organization with questions about their submission. The emails to all other people at SIFF are forwarded on to me, and then I receive eighteen copies of the same request for a fee waiver. I immediately, of course, want to know what film they are with, so I can watch out for it — and be angry with the filmmaker. If you have a question for the programming department, e-mail once — not every week — and please don't call to see if we've seen your film. We've either seen it or not, and if we have questions for you, we'll get in touch.

Do you guys pay screening fees?

BETH: Not as a matter of course. There are of course exceptions, but the screenings at SIFF are a wonderful launching point for press and audiences — especially now that media people can just put reviews and info on Facebook or Twitter.

Do you offer jury prizes?

BETH: We do! For features, we have jury prizes for first- and second-time directors, and documentaries. For the short film competitions, we give jury prizes in narrative, animation, and documentary. We are an Academy-qualifying festival in both narrative and animation, so the jury winners in those categories are eligible, provided they jump through the rest of the Academy hoops, to apply for the Academy Award. For the last couple of years, our jury winner has been short listed.

DUSTIN: The New Directors Prize goes to films that, at the time of selection, were without U.S. distribution. The competition gives wonderful opportunities to connect and distribute the film with the jury. We also have the FIPRESCI Prize that is awarded by International Federation of Film Critics to celebrate new American cinema, and we have recognition prizes, including the WaveMaker award for excellence in youth filmmaking.

Do you think that being an Academy qualifier brings in additional films? Do you think it's important to filmmakers and audiences?

BETH: I do. I think that the opportunity to be considered for an Academy Award is a huge bonus. I've definitely seen short film submissions go up in the four years since we've been a qualifier.

For filmmakers accepted into the Festival, do you offer travel funds or lodging? What do you do for people who come to Seattle?

BETH: We try to offer some support for every feature film that gets in the Festival. We're not able to every year, but we really make an attempt for filmmakers in some way.

What elements do you think add up to make a successful film?

BETH: It's gotta have great a story. That's the number one thing — seriously. If you don't have a good story, it doesn't matter how good the production values are, and it doesn't matter if you have Angelina Jolie in your film. If it's not a good story, it's not going to be a good film. For me that's really the key to it. Then, of course, once you have a good story, all of the other elements should fall into place — the acting has to be good and believable, and everything has to be in there for a reason.

Are there certain film conventions that trigger your "I love this! I want to love this film!" response?

DUSTIN: You know, I don't know. For myself, there's a feeling that comes with watching a film. Just because it's a Swedish vampire movie, doesn't mean that all Swedish vampire movies are my cup of tea.

Do you have any taboos or red flags — elements that instantly trigger a guttural "no way!" reaction?

BETH: Maybe excessive violence. I mean, I'm not opposed to violence in films if there's a reason for it, but just horrific violence for violence's sake to get a reaction? I think that's cowardly filmmaking. I like a good violent movie if it's got maturity. Oh, and I'm opposed to films that depict killing animals needlessly.

DUSTIN: Usually, sexuality or explicit sex isn't such a big deal.

BETH: It's actually a selling point.

DUSTIN: Yes, it's a selling point, but there have been a couple of times where we need to inform our audiences so that it's an 18+ audience. Other than that, I don't feel like we have many taboos.

What are your thoughts about premiere status? Is it important to SIFF?

BETH: It's important inasmuch as we love to be the place where people discover films. Our audiences love to be the ones to see a movie, but we're never going to choose a film just because it will be a premiere — especially over a film that is stronger, and that we are really excited to show our audiences.

DUSTIN: And I think from the filmmaker's standpoint, the chance to premiere at a larger festival is a big factor. Films that have a premiere status are usually rated a little higher by the audience, which gives more opportunities to connect with the community. I think that's true at any festival.

When choosing final selections, are you influenced by the accolades or awards a film has won elsewhere?

DUSTIN: Not in terms of what's actually programmed. I know if I'm looking for children's movies, I will look around to see what films have won awards, and I will be more apt to hunt them down. But, just because something won an award somewhere doesn't mean anything, really, in terms of whether a Seattle audience will like it or not. And it is really about how people here will connect, value, and take away from the film-going experience.

Are you influenced by big names in films?

BETH: Again we're not really influenced. More often than not, when a big actor is in a film, the property is usually pretty strong. But it still has to be a good film — just because it's got big names in it doesn't mean it's a better quality film.

So you wouldn't take a lousy film that had a big name over a really great film that features all no-names?

BETH: No, no! Definitely not. We'd love to have a big name in a film, and that's great! And we are a big, international film festival, so we show some more commercial films than most. But our focus has always been on independent, experimental, and documentaries.

Your audience is key. How much do their sensibilities play into your decision-making process?

DUSTIN: While I'm watching films, I'm not sure I'm really chewing on what the audience would think — I'm a little bit more in my world of wanting to connect emotionally with the work. Afterwards, I think about if the film is one the audience would come out to see, and/or be passionate about. When making the final selections, I'm always thinking about the audience. You have to be.

Have you ever programmed a film that you loved, but audiences thought was lackluster?

BETH: Well, yeah of course.

DUSTIN: There are times when you program something, and just because you cared for it, doesn't mean everyone in the audience will care for it.

Do you ever consider the thoughts of sponsors or donors when making selections?

BETH: We have some amazing sponsors that follow everything we do, and they don't ask us, "I think you should book this film!" But when we see a film that meets all of our qualifications for a good film then, yes, we would consider their needs. If we are waffling between two films of equal value, and one of them fits a sponsor perfectly, we would consider programming it. After all, the sponsors really do support so much of what we do in bringing the art of film to Seattle.

DUSTIN: Also, there are sponsors who are such a part of the Seattle fabric that we actively look for films that connect them to the Seattle audiences.

What role do distributors play in your selection process?

BETH: Over the years, we have come to a nice little understanding about what might be a really good film for Seattle audiences, and they understand the market and we understand the audience. The market and the audience are definitely two sides to the same coin.

After the selections are chosen, what is your process to actually schedule them into the 25-day event?

BETH: We definitely have a number of themed programs — there's our music program, which is all stories about or by musicians. And then we have documentary programs, sidebars and other focused programs. We tend to mix the films up quite a bit; we have a huge board — it's kind of an amazing thing to watch. We print out labels and start putting them on the board in slots. Last year we had just over 600 different slots. And, as we put them up, we look to make sure that all of the music films are not at the same time, or that we don't have three French films at the same time, or we can't have three Japanese and Cambodian films all at the same time, but maybe the Korean and Cambodian can be because one of them is LGBT. So for a few days, we sort this mess and try our best to make sure there are no obvious conflicts. We miss a couple every year, and afterwards think, "Oh yeah. That shouldn't have been at the same time, they have the same audience."

DUSTIN: When programming kids' material, we usually play them at 11:00 a.m. on Saturday and Sunday mornings. It would, of course, be surprising and a little illogical if we played them at midnight. Films for teens have to end by 9:30 p.m., especially on a school night. They just can't stay out any later.

While scheduling, do the limitations of time and venue affect the final lineup? Do you find that if you have too many of a particular theme, some have to be cut?

BETH: If we find a great film we're going to find a place for it. That said, when we're going into programming, we have to respect the limitations of time and venues — otherwise we'd end up with 475 feature films — and that's just unsustainable. So we have a little bit of a quota system. For our themes, we do not place limits on the number of films for each one. We can be flexible there.

Obviously you're the biggest festival in Seattle. How many other festivals are there in your area? Do you collaborate with these events?

BETH: There are about fifteen other festivals in Seattle, mostly created by community groups or niche festivals. And yes, we collaborate a lot. We act as curators for some of them, and more than that, we operate a year-round venue which most of the festivals in town use as part of their screenings, SIFF Cinema. Having space available for others is definitely part of our mission. It's really important to work in tandem with other festivals, because there are a lot of films out there, and the more independent and foreign films people see, the more we all benefit from the stronger audiences.

DUSTIN: And similar to what you have done in Washington DC, we participate in a group of festival directors and organizers in the Pacific Northwest that meets regularly to exchange information and learn about what is happening in the market.

What do you think is more important: schooling or story telling?

BOTH (in unison): Storytelling.

Ha ha! With the recent proliferation of film schools, do you think the quality of films has improved?

DUSTIN: Film schools create connections. There are not a lot of people who will go out and start making a film without any training. I think people in film schools are in more control and create more successful films.

Okay, a film has been accepted and the filmmaker is coming to SIFF. What should they do to make the most of their experience?

BETH: The more the filmmaker can do to reach out to the community, the better. Before they arrive, they should check in with the press department. But when they are here, they should be meeting people. They should be meeting people who might produce their next film; they should be out there doing grassroots publicity; they should ask what people think of their film. One of the things about SIFF is that we have audiences that are keen on talking to filmmakers — and are very active in the Q&A sessions. Not just the standard "how long, how much, what camera" questions, but thoughtful ones questioning artistic decisions or character development. Our audiences really consume film — they don't just watch.

DUSTIN: We have a program to take filmmakers to local schools — it can be colleges to elementary schools — and it's not just an opportunity to connect students to the filmmaking world. It is a great opportunity to reach a younger crowd, and explore what future audiences will be expecting.

What's the nicest compliment you have received from a filmmaker?

BETH: Honestly, when someone tells you, "Thank you. It's an amazing festival," it doesn't get much better than that. They realize they connected with the audiences and that their films have made an impact.

DUSTIN: I don't recall a particular quote, but when I watch filmmakers at the

Q&A and see in their eyes that they made that connection, it is a special moment.

What's the worst thing a filmmaker has ever said to you?

BETH: A few years ago, we had a film about a street musician with mental health issues. Unfortunately, the projector overheated halfway through the film, and we needed to bring in a technician to fix the problem. After about 45 minutes, we got the screening running again and the film continued with a much smaller, and slightly drunker, audience. Then after the film at the Q&A, the subject of the movie, who had not seen it until the screening, stood up and accused the filmmaker that she was lied to about the project, and stormed out. When it was all over (thankfully) the filmmaker cornered me and told me, "That was the worst experience of my life." I don't blame him.

Do you guys have a secret blacklist? And how does one get on it?

DUSTIN: You have to run a film festival and be named Jon Gann.

Ha ha! Is that why my films never play at SIFF? Now I know!

DUSTIN: We don't have a secret blacklist — at least nothing on paper. I'm sure there have been people over the years who behaved badly, and we would be hesitant to extend an invitation for them to attend. Again, we need to think about our audience and the experience they will have. Do we want them connecting with a filmmaker who might be unpleasant?

What three words best describe what you do?

BETH:

1. Inspire.
2. Educate.
3. Entertain.

DUSTIN: Which is exactly why I got into this field.

Lastly, if you could give would be entrants one last piece of advice, what would it be?

BETH: Edit your film. We really see so many features that are just 15 minutes too long, or shorts that need a few minutes trimmed.

DUSTIN: Don't be afraid to kill your babies — taking out scenes that you love, but don't add to the overall story.

I would also add that one of the best things to do is get involved with a festival and become a pre-screener or programmer. If you really understood the process — and have the opportunity to see the films that don't make the cut — you have a major advantage over other filmmakers.

"WOMAN ON TIGHTROPE" AMY ETTINGER

Executive Director, Scottsdale International Film Festival

About the Festival:

- Founded in 2001, the Scottsdale International Film Festival is a destination event and catalyst for connecting diverse filmmakers from around the world with film lovers in a fresh, thought provoking, and enduring community of support.
- 5-day event for general audiences; event targeting local film enthusiasts
- Web: scottsdalefilmfestival.com

It is fitting that Amy Ettinger, the founder and Executive Director of the Scottsdale International Film Festival, was born abroad in Orleans, France. Ettinger's love of film, especially foreign film, turned a sleepy Arizona film community into a vibrant center for premiering the best in foreign films. In 2010 for the Festival's 10th anniversary, Ettinger landed a coup of major importance with the U.S. premiere of *The Girl Who Kicked the Hornet's Nest.* Partnering for four years with the Toronto Film Festival starting in 2002, Ettinger secured appearances with renowned actors such as Leslie Ann Warren & Jennifer Tilly, and with directors such as John Sayles, Mike Leigh, and Ted Kotcheff. Before creating the Scottsdale International Film Festival, Amy founded the Out Far! Lesbian and Gay Film Festival which had a 10 year run.

What's the history of the Scottsdale International Film Festival, and how did you get involved in it?

I'd been running the Out Far! Lesbian and Gay Film Festival in Phoenix for years. While in Paris on vacation I left a movie theater along the Champs-Élysées when it struck me that I should create an international festival. Too much incredible product never gets to our nook of the world. The first year of the international festival occurred twelve days after 9/11. Needless to say, I was a little nervous at the timing, but it worked out well, and we have thrived ever since.

That is interesting. I also attended a start-up festival the week after 9/11, and the community came together in a way that was magical. It is still one of my favorite festival experiences.

I think that in critical times, people need a release. The outpouring from the community was heartwarming and healing.

What's your background?

I have a background in music. I was a musician for many years, performing concerts to put myself through school, where I majored in radio and television production. I was brought up in Chicago where the arts flourish. But when I moved to Arizona in 1976, I noticed a drought of both water and the arts. So, I threw myself into the fray, and over the years, I morphed and came out as a festival director.

Before you created the Festival, did you attend many other film events?

Oh, yes. I also gave my time to film festivals for ten years here. I've been to numerous festivals — LA's OutFest, the insideout GLBT Festival in Toronto, Desperado Film Festival, Greater Phoenix Jewish Film Festival, Phoenix Film Festival, and the International Costume & Fashion Film Festival (FCM) in Paris.

Now that you're a programmer, do you find you're still going to festivals?

I still haven't made it to Sundance, and only get to the Phoenix Film Festival every other year or so. I futilely plan to go to Seattle and Toronto every year, but haven't because those events are too close to our deadline. I wish I could get to more, but there never seems to be enough time or money.

What's your favorite film festival and why? Or, is there a festival that you admire and learn from?

My favorite festival is the Toronto Film Festival (TIFF) and for many years they were this festival's partner. My aunt was a volunteer with TIFF when they started. She prevailed upon them to meet with me in 2001 and I made a presentation, and lo and behold, they took me dead seriously! We worked together for four years running and they mentored me in festival production. It was a partnership that really changed the focus and ultimate viability of the Scottsdale Film Festival.

Can you describe your submission and selection process? How do I apply, and then what happens when my entry gets there?

For unsolicited films, we have a total of four judges including me. Everything that comes in is screened by at least one of the other judges. They clear out the amateurish projects so that I am not saddled watching films which are not up to our standards.

Films that we invite automatically go to the second round. And I am the second round. I'm looking for films that have top-notch production values. There isn't a filter in my head that says, "Oh, this is inappropriate," or, "Oh, this is too accessible and too family-friendly." The process has more to do with finding an interesting story told well and those which possess strong production values.

We receive many films with a really interesting premise, but they're made very badly — inauthentic acting, or poor production, camera and lighting. Conversely, we get some films with phenomenal production values, but stories that are not all that engaging.

With only 35 to 40 films in the final lineup, I am trying to get a balance of continents, countries, ethnicity, religion, comedy, drama, and narrative — it's a juggling act. At the end, I come out with a mosaic of film, which is our goal: I want people to walk away saying that everything they saw was unique in some way — different from the last, and different from the next.

Big festivals like Palm Springs have many films available to them – and the venues to show many. We do not have that luxury, so I am always looking for film with a discerning eye. For example, I try to get the Oscar-potential films. I watch most of them, and out of fifty or sixty, we might end up exhibiting five to nine of those Oscar contenders.

Okay, so you say high production value is really important to you. If you had a film with a great story and great acting, but the picture looked like it was done with a VHS camera, would you consider it?

Our audience is extremely high-brow and feels entitled. They're like the Palm Springs audience in a lot of ways, so we cater to them. Choosing film is a very delicate balance, because we don't want to alienate the core patron— this highly educated, well-traveled, affluent, audience wants to see films from around the world. At the same time, I want to find new independent domestic films to put into the mix, and lure a younger demographic. Once we get an audience, we keep them. We have very little attrition. We have grown nearly every year. Everything is on a case-by-case basis. But if something looks bad on a screener it will likely not make the cut.

How long is your submission and selection process?

I start in January and cut off in July for submissions. Generally speaking, by the beginning of July, I have a pretty good idea of what I'm doing. If a film comes in close to the final deadline late in the month, it's going to have to be a Hail Mary pass for it to get it in. We've had a couple of films come in on deadline day, and have killed ourselves to fit them in because they were just that good. But it's torture when that happens because we have the whole schedule nearly put to bed by the time those films arrive.

So, do you watch the films in their entirety?

We make sure every single film that's been submitted with a fee is watched. We will watch 40 minutes minimum of every film. By minute 40, if it's just excruciatingly awful, if it's just a train wreck, if there's just too much amateur production, I give my programmers permission to stop watching. And you know what? They very rarely take the out. They really do watch every single film all the way through, no matter how much they hate the experience.

Do you charge a submission fee? What is your purpose for charging one?

We have four price points over the course of the submission period starting at $20. We didn't used to charge the fees, but implemented them as a quality control measure. And in fact, we raised the prices this year because we're still trying to deter subpar submissions. I'm not trying to insult anyone in particular, but we get a lot of, "You can't be serious about this, did you really think anybody is ever going to play this film anywhere on any screen?" submissions. Asking people for the fee means to me they're much more serious about their product if they decide to pay for submission. Now, this only affects about 50 filmmakers a year. We never charge a fee to the 400 or so we invite.

That is few. So you watch and invite 400 films?

Here's the thing: of the 400 that I reach out to, 200 might get back to me with a screener. We often do not get responses because of language barriers, or they are films that a distributor doesn't want to show in this market, or the distributor does not want to show in our time frame, or they are price prohibitive.

We accept blind submissions through Withoutabox almost entirely to discover one or two films a year.

A good exception to the previous comment is *Sons of Provo*. At the time, I was the only programmer (I was the only everything back then), and I watched the first several minutes and thought, "this is so bad, like a lousy *South Park* episode." And then all of a sudden, it turned into the most fantastic, tongue-in-cheek mockumentary, poking good-natured fun at Mormonism. It was a satirical musical about a Mormon boy band — written and performed by Mormons. I love it! We ended up marketing the film heavily in Mesa, a local city here with a large Mormon population, and tons of teenagers showed up. It was a great success. One of the film's leads was a teen Mormon heartthrob, and he ended up doing very well. Just a couple of years ago he starred in the Broadway revival cast of *Hair*, and is now engaged to Audra McDonald!

Do you take online screeners?

We just started taking them in 2011. It's not terrific — none of us like watching these films on computer. We have an eight-foot screen for the express purpose of watching films so that we can see how they'll play in a big room. So when we're forced to watch something in miniature, it definitely forces us to use our focus and work harder.

Do you give feedback to filmmakers?

Yes, but only for films which are accepted. I used to give feedback for those we did not accept until filmmakers started becoming defensive and abusive. Then I ultimately decided, "I don't need this abuse and the arguments." I had worked diligently to be diplomatic, but when filmmakers called to scream at me, or send me vitriolic emails, I thought, "Life is too short. I really, literally, do not have the time for this distraction."

Do you find media kits helpful when making decisions?

Not at all. If we accept the film, we'll go back and ask for an EPK [electronic press kit.] It depends on how much marketing we can provide a particular film.

Do you pay screening fees?

We pay screening fees on a case-by-case basis. There's a festival that shall remain nameless, that's never paid a dime for screening fees. You can really see it — they've got quantity, but the quality's is atrocious. I'm doing what it takes to create a jewel of a boutique film festival, and I can't do that without paying for programming. I think the audience gets what they've paid for, and the Festival gets what it pays for.

I wish we didn't have that line item — it's one of our biggest budget items, but ethically, I cannot justify not paying filmmakers for their films. Now, with all that said, we would never pay a screening fee to a major studio for one of their entries. They don't need our measly $500 anyway.

Do you offer jury prizes?

No, but we have an audience award — and it's only for the best film. Last year, we presented our first ever Artistic Diversity Award to John Sayles. The audience was fully engaged in the film, and he was fully engaged and humbled while accepting the award. We hope to be able to do that every year with a different director.

Are you Academy considered? Do you think it matters to filmmakers or audiences?

No. And I don't know. I think it matters more to filmmakers than our audience.

For filmmakers who are accepted, do you offer travel funds or lodging?

On a case-by-case basis, yes. Our budget is very small, but usually, we end up bringing out one or two filmmakers. Every year there's a filmmaker who is truly independent, who's done it all on their own. We try to help them out. But we can't do it for everyone; we don't have the budget yet. We're crawling up the totem pole in terms of funding, but it's a really slow creep.

What are your thoughts about premiere status?

I want them! I want as many as I can get. And on occasion we get a world or US premiere, but mostly local or Arizona premieres. It is one of the things Toronto drummed into my head year after year.

I thought it was just absurd that I would premiere a film that would open next week, or next month. Who in their right mind would want to pay $10 admission to see it if they could see it for two or three dollars cheaper in a week or a month? I really had my nose up in the air about it, but TIFF convinced me that it is a great marketing device, and a terrific way to lure people who would otherwise not come to the Festival for small films. Fast-forward a few years, and it is one of the best decisions we adopted.

Are you influenced by accolades a film received at other festivals, or is it not really applicable because you're taking mostly premieres?

Accolades mean a lot to me, but I don't think they mean anything to my audience. The more laurels I see on a film, the more I start paying attention as I build the list of films that I want dibs on.

Are you influenced by big names in movies?

I am because my audience is influenced. You know I've got a business to run, so as much as I'd like to be all about the artsy aspect of it, I've got to pay the bills. My PR people say to me every year, "Give us some names!" They want some recognizable talent to use for film critics, and to get stories placed in the local papers.

Would you take a mediocre film with a name over a film with a better story, but no celebrity attached?

I probably wouldn't have to wind up making that decision. Thankfully, I've never been in a spot where I had to pick one over the other.

A couple of years ago, Mike Leigh was touring with *Happy Go Lucky*, and my PR firm mistakenly told him that my closing night was two nights after my actual closing night. So, I ended up having two closing nights — I mean I'll do what it takes to make it work. It was a great decision and produced a standing-room-only event. We unfortunately turned away 400 people due to a sold-out house, the Q&A lasted an hour and fifteen minutes — and nobody budged.

So, how important is your audience, ultimately, in your final process and selection?

They're always sitting on my left shoulder, and my artistic sensibility is sitting on my right. Last year, I programmed all of the Global Film Initiative's 2011 catalog. And wow, that's a line-up of some pretty difficult film — many of them don't have a soundtrack — but that's why I got into this industry. I played three of those films three times and really pushed the hell out of them, but very few people showed up. That's my right shoulder — my artistic side — forcing the issue on why I started the Festival in the first place.

And then on my left shoulder is *Like Crazy* because Anton Yelchin and Felicity Jones were attending, or *Amigo* because John Sayles agreed to attend. I know my audience is going to turn out for those films. Sam Shepard in Blackthorn? Heck yeah! I didn't like the film, but my audience did. It's 50-50 — I'm true to myself, and I'm true to my audience.

So have you ever programmed a film that you loved, but your audience just could not connect with?

The *Werckmeister Harmonies*, by Bela Tarr. That's just one, of a million examples! I'll probably book more Tarr in the future anyhow!

Can you share lessons learned from this?

I learn that I'm going to take a bath on a few films. I don't like to see empty rooms, and I don't really have the budget to lose money with every film. But I want to score a victory every now and again with someone or several people who walk out of a theater and say, "I'm not sure what I just saw, but it was fantastic!" They don't always have to get it, but I don't always have to bow down, or pander. So, yeah, I'll always program at least one where a few people come up to me afterward and ask me what the hell I was thinking. I'm sorry they didn't like it, but there were a couple of other people in that room who did.

Are you ever influenced by sponsors or donors into making a decision?

I unequivocally refuse influence pedaling. That said, I do have funders who have asked me to consider films. I programmed one film in the instance when it completely merited a slot. I have also told the same funders "no" on other requested films and they were fine with my decision. Even if they were not fine with my decision, I will not be pressured into making a programming choice by funders.

Are you ever influenced by what distributors want you to take?

I wish the distributors were that forward. With one particular distributor, there's very rarely been a year where we haven't had an argument. He wants me to take this, that, or the other thing and I only want one of the three. He yells at me and he tells me how crazy I am. In the end I prevail. On the other hand, another distributor has a fantastic memory of what we have shown and our audience composition, which means they will only offer what they think is appropriate.

When you ultimately schedule your festival, and you're putting it altogether, how do you figure out what goes where? And when you figure out the puzzle, do you sometimes find that you have to jettison a film, or bring another in?

I've never jettisoned a film because it doesn't fit in or it isn't fitting into the programming. I'm creating a mosaic, so I don't see the point.

Putting together the schedule, however, is an exercise in clever problem solving. It is probably one of the more complicated aspects of running a festival. I might try to bait the audience by screening a popular film early in the morning, but that can backfire. There are definitely films which are best played at specific times of the day: family during the day, sexy or exceedingly violent later at night. Also, there are certain distributors who require a specific outbound shipping date which forces me to program those films on the weekend. There are other films that cannot arrive until weekdays. Quite a few decisions are made based upon timing and availability of the films themselves.

Earlier, you mentioned strong story and production values as major influencers. What other elements do you think make a successful festival film?

That's such an open-ended question. Some of the most successful films in our festival have been what I consider "familiar" — a fresh perspective on an old story. There is that adage that there are no new stories, this film is just a French version of such-and-such, or an Italian version of another story I've seen or read. I think that familiarity adds to people's enjoyment of what they're watching. It's something they can relate to, something that speaks to them, something that is eerily reminiscent of something already in their heart, or soul, or mind.

Then are those times when I program films and during the initial viewing, I think, "Wow! That's just stupendous! I've never heard, seen, thought, conceived of that particular story line. How novel, how unusual, how creative." Although they were not Festival films, I'm still wrestling with *Inception* and *Memento*. I probably need to see those films three more times before I get my arms around them. Christopher Nolan has the propensity to weave a story that's just perplexing and hard to follow, but in the end the payoff is that you just spent two hours being surprised.

Are there any red flags or taboos which make you think "I can't...I'm not watching more of this?"

It's happened very few times. I can be very experimental and very broad-minded, so there are few films I would not sit through. A few years back, we did have a film which five of us could not get through.

As for taboos, I think it's all about context. *The Woodsman* with Kevin Bacon is about a pedophile, but the story is strong and engaging. If we had the opportunity at the time I would have programmed it in a minute. We showed *13 Tzameti* in 2006, a film which features a lot of violence through terrifying rounds of Russian roulette. It is an intense film — so much so, that some audience members had to leave the theater to clear their heads. One woman came to me in the lobby asked why I would program such a film. I responded that while the film was about a very difficult subject matter, I am not a censor. The theater sold very well for both screenings — almost a sell out, so it obviously resonated with many audience members.

What do you think is more important — schooling, or storytelling?

I actually don't think one is more important than the other.

What effect do you think the recent proliferation of film schools has had on films that are coming across your desk?

I wish that the professors would stop allowing films to be made featuring guns and knives. In the many film school submissions we have received everyone's being killed by a gun or a knife.

I agree with you. When I was in film school I had a writing teacher who argued, "If you have to kill someone to resolve your film, you don't know how to write." What thematic trends have you seen in the last year or so?

Thinking back to last season, we received many films concerning the Eastern bloc and all its grimness. Now we're on to the cycle of Middle Eastern war, the power of death, and the resulting sorrow. I have sometimes wanted to slit my wrists.

Has your job as a program jaded your opinion of film in general, or has it expanded your appreciation?

Oh my gosh, expanded it! You know, before I started the Festival, I got up every morning of my life for years and just enjoyed films. Now, with the exception of some asinine Hollywood/Seth Rogan-esque vehicles, I really appreciate film and the points of view filmmakers are putting forth.

What's the nicest thing a filmmaker has ever said to you?

The director Ted Kotcheff said, "This is the best run festival I've ever attended."

What's the worst thing a filmmaker's ever said to you?

When I used to give feedback to rejected films, someone once screamed that I had my head up my ass and that I didn't know what I was doing. I understood that they were unhappy, but I expected that they would take the feedback with graciousness. I was obviously naïve.

Do you have a secret blacklist?

No. I wouldn't even know where to begin. I don't hold grudges, but I am cautious about being burned by the same person more than once.

Do you have a favorite success story?

Very early on, we had the premieres of three films, including *Babel* with Brad Pitt and *The Queen* with Helen Mirren. They gave us a tremendous amount of credibility, and we garnered a lot of respect from the media and from our audience. We sold out the one screening and sadly had to turn people away from *Babel*. People I never would have thought would attend lined up around the block. There was a lot of ticket swapping going on.

We were also one of four festivals in the entire country to get the unedited version of *The Kite Runner* before it was pulled by the studio to deal with the PR nightmare concerning the kids from Afghanistan. Our audience really lucked out with that one.

If you could give would-be entrants one piece of advice, what would it be?

Just read the submission guidelines! Read them all — it's really not that much. I don't want to sound trite, but it's important because you don't know how many times I wind up saying, "These people don't read!" It might save you money — I've had dozens of filmmakers submit short subjects — even though our rules say we do not screen any short films.

Yeah, I'm with you on this one. So, what three words best describe what you do?

Woman on tightrope.

"WATCH. FEEL. THINK." J'AIMEE SKIPPON-VOLKE

Festival Director, Byron Bay International Film Festival (Australia)

About the Festival:

- Founded in 2007, BBFF is a large competitive regional New South Wales film festival with a high global profile — providing the Northern Rivers, one of Australia's most active film hubs, with a strong international platform that highlights filmmaking as a key creative industry in our region and our state.
- 10-day event for general audiences with niche programming to showcase surf, environmental, human rights/social justice, and spiritual films.
- Website: bbff.com.au

J'aimee grew up in the world of International Television with both parents (who were originally from NYC) working as Directors and Producers. Born in Australia, her family moved to New Zealand and then eventually settled in London, England. J'aimee has a solid working history in Pre-, Post- and Production Services for Film and Television as well as Event Management. After moving to Byron Bay in Australia, J'aimee built upon her experience working in post production in London's Soho to co-found GreenhouseFX, an animation and effects facilities company.

J'aimee worked behind the scenes during the inaugural Byron Bay Film Festival. With years of experience in film and television production, J'aimee's knowledge of the film industry, marketing and business came into play. Together with her exceptional organizational skills, she engaged in the challenge of taking the Festival to the next level in terms of growth and exposure. J'aimee also programmed and directed the Activating Human Rights Film Festival which was held as part of a Human Rights Conference held every five years.

What is the history of the Byron Bay Film Festival, and how did you get involved with it?

Byron Bay and the northern New South Wales region are home to a substantial number of filmmakers. It holds the third largest community of filmmakers in Australia, which is amazing considering that it's a regional area. In response to this, the inaugural Byron Bay Film Festival in February 2006 focused on screening the back catalogue of our local filmmakers' work plus other Australian films. However, the immediate and enthusiastic audience feedback from this festival motivated the management team to expand the screenings to include international films, a positive drawing card for an expanding international audience.

The first festival was created by a team of four local filmmakers and Greg Aitken, our Executive Producer. Greg was looking to fill a hole in his venue's season. One of the four filmmakers on that team was my partner, Osvaldo Alfaro. I worked behind the scenes with the collective in a minor fashion, helping out with data entry and random office tasks to lend a hand.

After the 2006 festival, Greg asked if I would manage the Festival, as he knew I could see that the full potential wasn't being reached. I had put in a funding application for a documentary idea, and said if it was funded I was off to make films, and if not, I would give the Festival a go. At the time I was a stay-at-home mom with young children and so had spare time and an interest in keeping myself busy and working in the world of film.

Did you attend festivals when you were younger?

No, but I was a huge fan of indie and alternative cinema as a teen. I grew up in central London in the 1980s and the Scala was my stomping ground. I also lived very close to the ICA (Institute of Contemporary Arts), and as a teen, watched lots of art house films there, too.

What is your background?

I changed jobs a lot, and when I was in TV and film, I couldn't make up my mind whether I wanted to work in production or post-production. My partner, Ossie (who is BBFF's Technology Director,) introduced me to the medium of short films and I felt the heart which I believed was lacking from TV.

I had also been involved with underground dance clubs in Sydney in the 1990s, and I have brought what I learned about creating a loyal following into the Festival.

How many festivals do you get to now?

Not enough. Australia's a large place, so probably only four a year. I am making an effort to attend at least one major film festival a year. This year, it was Edinburgh.

What is your favorite festival and why?

My favorite festival is not a festival at all. I love the Asia Pacific Screen Awards, an event to honor and promote and preserve the cultures of the Asia-Pacific through the medium of film. It's a wonderful event, encouraging cultural and artistic identity, and forges connections between the countries and filmmakers involved. It's held just up the road from Byron on the Gold Coast. The quality of films is outstanding, and although I'm not usually patriotic or particularly proud of Australian culture, it makes me feel really positive that this is an Australian-driven initiative. The quality of films nominated and the talent of the filmmakers showcased are just phenomenal. Literally, the best the world has to offer.

So, describe your screening and judging process. I mail my disc in, what goes on from there?

Okay, we have a very lovely submissions coordinator who manages film arrivals and adding to the database. That is a task in itself!

It's only as the Festival has grown that I've stopped watching every single film in its entirety. Back when we had 240 entries, it wasn't an issue to watch them all. Now we're up to about 900 entries, and it's just impossible for me to do.

The Festival is still small, so in addition to programming, I am also the events manager, so it became difficult for me to put 100 percent of my time into watching every film. We developed a system where team members watch all of the films and provide feedback for me. The team started with people whose opinions I trust, or who reflect what the audience especially wants. Bit by bit, we're developing a system where films go through this team of people before it comes to me.

Yet, I still will not trust myself to give over to all of the feedback enough to not watch a bit of the films myself. So I still watch a portion of every film, even if team members said, "Whatever you do, don't watch this film." I want to check, because opinions are so different. Some of the team are in their sixties, and they have a very different viewpoint than a younger viewer, while others are wildly optimistic and innocent, and come back saying, "It's lovely and beautiful," and I find that sort of feedback to be vacuous. So you know, I have a degree of trust in my screeners, but then, at the same time, I want to make sure for myself.

How many people are on the team?

About eight core people, with some floaters for niche categories. We program a lot of surfing and environmental films. Our floaters for the surf films are called the "surfboard." They are a great bunch, and have really helped me to better understand surf culture. Even so, some of these guys have been in the professional surfing circuit since they were 17 years old and they're now in their sixties. They know what surfers want, and in order to bring authenticity to what we do, we have to run films by people who really understand the niche.

Often, team members will double as judges as well, so I'm sort of using the judges as well—particularly with the surf category — to help me narrow down what the end selection is. Two birds with one stone.

And does this initial team watch the films in their entirety?

Yup. Well, I do ask them to. If a feature film is clearly not good, I don't think anyone's doing any favors by watching it through once they determine that it is not worth continuing. So if they turn to read a book or surf the net, I understand.

The thing I really noticed over the years, is the quality of the technicians [crew] has gotten better. It used to be that you could spot a film that wasn't going to work because the camera work would be shoddy, or the sound would be trailing. Now, the technicians just excel at their crafts. Now I am much more aware of bad acting, bad script, or bad directing.

What type of criteria do you score or comment on?

We have a rating sheet where screeners rate a film on a scale of one to five with half-points. We score on story, script, direction, production values, entertainment value, acting, and audience appeal. One of the things we're looking for at all times is the audience appeal. We program very much for our local community — it's very unique, and they have many varied interests.

Of these eight screeners, how many of them are film professionals? Do you think it is important that they are?

I think, probably three. Its not a big issue because the audience on the whole isn't. Although we do have a very high population of filmmakers in our area, we program for film lovers.

I'm very envious of people with short film festivals.

Why is that?

Because of the sheer number of films. Having 900 films that go on for 15 or 20 minutes as opposed to 500 features — often over two hours long. The process of getting through them is obviously that much easier.

Dream on. The films might be shorter, but the scrutiny is the same. And I think that filmmakers are more apt to make and invest time and money in a crummy short than a crummy feature. Do you charge a submission fee? Why?

Yes, we do. Because we basically need every penny we can get to pull this thing off. The Festival is run with a lot of love — it's practically entirely volunteer driven — and we like to show our filmmakers a good time. Every penny we earn goes towards the actual event. We used to have a fundraiser, but discovered that it cost us more to pull off than we collected. We are very conservative with any money we spend.

Do you give feedback to the filmmakers?

We used to, but no, not anymore. We release our list of programmed films very close to the start of the Festival, so filmmakers wanted feedback during the last days of preparation — when we are the craziest. Then there is the workload involved in actually giving people feedback after the event, because by that time, you've forgotten their film, and there is little time to re-watch since we are already working on the next year.

And of course, there are the filmmakers who didn't want to hear the feedback that they received — and complained, often in the most unprofessional ways. When someone's being difficult, it makes you wonder why you would even provide such a service if that is the thanks you will get. Those people spoiled our giving feedback to the people who might've been more open to it.

I've decided there's definitely a sort of talent-to-humility ratio. The most talented filmmakers are the nicest and easy to deal with, and those with the least talent are the ones who give you the most amount of shit.

Ha ha! Well, if it's any consolation, you are not the first person to say that either on or off the record. So, I think that most of us would agree. Do you find that media kits are helpful in the decision making process?

No, but they're incredibly helpful once we've actually been doing the selections. Sometimes I'll be reading through the synopsis beforehand. But very often I'll be somewhat flying blindly, barely having a proper flight visa when I watch with the screeners.

And what's the biggest mistake a filmmaker can make when submitting to the Festival?

A disk that doesn't work. Or is shipped improperly so it arrives broken or scratched. This is less of a mistake than a pet peeve, but I can't stand wasting money on overnight shipping. You can always send us an online screener, and the Australian post is very swift. It just seems like a waste of money and resources.

And of course, entering the right category. If you enter the wrong category, you could miss out on winning an award. We have a Young Australian Filmmaker Award, but so many filmmakers don't enter the category because they don't read the rules or are not careful when filling out the online form.

I'm with you 100 percent. You obviously like online screeners. Have you had any problems with them?

I think we receive about fifty percent of our screeners online. Sometimes one or two of them won't work. Also, I wish Withoutabox's system was upgraded so it worked more like Vimeo or other services where we can scroll forward and back with more ease.
For those who submit on DVD, we ask for two discs because, inevitably, one will fail. But this means we can have up to 2,000 DVDs in the office. Byron Bay is a very environmentally friendly place, so the whole idea of all those discs, and the cost of delivery and the expense of the packaging is a bit abhorrent.

Do you pay screening fees?

We started with the policy of not paying screening fees because we literally could not afford to do it. Since then, we have offered a few films which we really wanted to program (it would bring a large audience, it was through a major distributor, there was no other way we could get it), but I feel like it's creating an inconsistency and disparity between the filmmakers — someone is worthy and someone is not. That doesn't sit very well with me. I'd love to be at a position where we have the funds to actually pay all filmmakers. We are always revisiting this and trying to figure out the best for everyone involved.

For accepted filmmakers, do you offer travel funds or lodging? What do you offer them when they get there?

The policy is that we offer free housing to the people who travel the farthest on a first-come, first-served basis. We try to house everyone who indicates they are in need, but we don't necessarily house Australians. Some people end up on a waiting list, and we offer them heavily discounted accommodations at area hotels.

What are your thoughts about premier status? Are you often influenced to take a film because it's a premier?

If two films are equally worthy — that's when premier status is taken into account. We're in a small area about 500 miles away from Sydney. There's not a massive amount of films that have come through the area, even though we have a couple of art house cinemas. Premier status means a lot more to large urban audiences than it does to ours. Ours are grateful to see something new and exciting — whether or not it played in Melbourne or London or New York already.

Are you influenced at all by what accolades or awards a film received at another festival?

The thing that interests me is audience awards. I think that they're the ones that must have made the most impact. Winning best film of the year, or best thematic feature, or any of those kinds of awards come down to taste of the judge or the flavor of that festival. I've seen award-winning films elsewhere that have very little appeal to our audience.

I'm very audience-focused. I take my voice out of the process and just pretend I'm Joe or Barb. What do they want to see? What is their interest?

Are you influenced by big names in films?

Well, it makes it an easier sell to the audience, but I have also seen films with big names that don't necessarily have that edge. Again, a bit like the premier status, if it's up against a film with the exact same merit, and it's got a name, then that's obviously going to be a selling point for it. But it's not going to influence me to take a film that clearly isn't going to work for our festival just because it has a famous name attached.

Have you ever programmed a film that you loved, but the audience just didn't get it?

No, but I've programmed features that I didn't get and the audience loved. That's the whole "taking my personal feeling out of it." I leave my personal taste for the shorts — that's one bit when my sensibilities come through.

How important are the thoughts of your sponsors or your donors when making decisions?

They don't come into it at all because, unfortunately, we don't have large enough sponsors that they can buy up our opinion. I'm joking. Byron is a very unique community: we're very political, very left wing, very green, and very active in a lot of environmental and social justice issues.

Do distributors play any role in your selection process?

No. Until a couple of years ago, 99 percent of the films submitted didn't have a distributor attached. Now, more and more are represented, which has become a small issue. We used to have people who worked for distributors on our judging panels. Now, we have to make sure that either the judges have no financial gain in making recommendations, or we just look for other screening team members.

How do you ultimately schedule your selections? You have eight days and 200 films and limited numbers of screens. How do you put them all together?

I've got a master Excel sheet that I did up three years ago. It has the time of each session, and I basically start sticking the features I know I want in first. Then I start playing with the shorts that I know will play with the features. Then it just becomes a numbers game where you're moving things around to make the timings match.

And so, when you plug stuff in, do you find that affects the films you ultimately select? Do any have to be cut because of time or space considerations?

Well, it might affect programming shorts. In Withoutabox, we assign every film a flag: green for "definitely yes," red for "probably no, but I want to encourage the filmmaker," yellow for "let's revisit," and black for a flat-out "no." While I want to show all of the green ones, I sometimes have to pick a yellow because the theme of the short works better with the feature. Also, we try to show local films, so sometimes, a yellow pick will take out a green one.

Do you curate from other film festivals?

I look at what's on at other festivals. This past year, I went to Edinburgh and found a couple of films there that I really liked, and wanted to bring back. I don't know if I necessarily curate, but I look for standout films.

Do you consult with other festival programmers?

I talk to many through online forums or on the phone. If they recommend something, I will look at it. I'll also ask alumni filmmakers if they have seen a film which will play well here. But ultimately, the film will go through the same process as any other submission.

How many other festivals are in Byron Bay? Do they influence the films you select?

We are the biggest in the area. There are a few touring festivals that come through — that is a new trend in which bigger metropolitan events are reaching out to smaller communities to show their top picks. Some of our neighboring towns have other festivals, but they are a good 35 kilometers away and the event is smaller.

We are happy to program a film that has played one of these events, as long as it's going to work for the program. Again, two films being equal, we will go with the one that's fresh.

What elements do you think add up to make a successful film? What do you think are the elements that just make you stand up and say, "Yes!"

You know what I think? I think a filmmaker should take the exact same approach that I take to the Festival: Make that film with the audience in mind.

It is easy to miss the mark and be over indulgent with unnecessary scenes, characters or dialogue. Or pretty shots that don't add to the storytelling. When I've given feedback to filmmakers, I've had some come back and say, "Yeah, you're right. But this shot that took us all day to get, so we had a lot of trouble letting go of it." I think the best films are when the filmmaker actually lets go of all of their personal baggage, and focuses on making the best possible film they can, rather than the one to prove that they are creative.

I also admit, I tend to rate the teary-eye factor highly. We once had a film where I looked at the audience and all I could see was a sea of white. I'm like, "what's that?" Then I realized it was tissues — the whole place was crying because the film was so powerful. It wasn't manipulation, it was just that people felt so moved by what on the screen. Now, that is great storytelling.

Are there any taboos or themes you just cannot show?

I'm a very open-minded person, but I cannot in good conscience program something that my audience will really hate, such as superfluous adult content.

The other thing that I'm not into is unnecessary violence. I don't know if filmmakers are watching too much CSI, but people are killed off without any reason. That turns me off. Sometimes you'll have a really great story, and a filmmaker thinks they're building the tension by throwing these scenes in, but actually, they do nothing for the film.

I agree. Which do you think is more important, schooling or storytelling?

Definitely it's the ability to tell a story. Definitely. And filmmakers either have it or they don't.

I've seen plenty of movies that come from film schools that are very average and very bland. I've also seen films from self-taught filmmakers that will blow your mind. This younger generation that's been brought up on the Internet, and their brains work in a very different way than our generation: they go off in a different linear direction, and tell stories in a very fascinating way.

Do you think this type of storytelling matches the audience that's currently buying tickets?

That is the question of the year. I find, especially here, a lot of our audience is older. We're actively working towards creating new and younger audiences screening more surf films.

When a filmmaker comes to Byron Bay, what should they do to get the most out of the experience?

At the Festival we can only create so much press ourselves — the local papers are over-saturated with our releases and articles, and they're already publishing what they want from us. The best thing a filmmaker can do is actually get out there and promote themselves — putting their own articles in, offering themselves up to the local radio stations, and really making an effort to create a fan base.

Also, staying really sociable and networking as much as possible helps — and taking advantage of all the opportunities that are offered to you through the Festival. We set up many parties and other events for filmmakers to network with one another. While not everyone has to spend all their time socializing, those that are "out there" have this amazing festival experience versus people who kind of keep to themselves.

I often say that a film festival is very much like other festivals — a bunch of strangers come together and they have a shared experience — and then they go away friends. That's really what we're really trying to encourage at our event.

I agree. I was talking to someone else about how film festivals seem to have this ability to create new friendships, whether it's you standing in line for tickets and you just start talking to the person standing next to you, and the next thing you know you're having dinner...there's something about festivals that bring out the social aspects of people.

Yeah, very much.

Do you have a favorite success story? Maybe a film that played BBFF and ended up doing very well because of it? Or, a filmmaker who was encouraged by your festival to go on to greatness?

I think my favorite success story is more of a backwards thing, an Australian short film which had its world premiere in Berlin and won the Jury Special Mention. We had their Australian Premiere and they told us they'd made the film with us in mind.

Describe an incident that you would have considered to be less than successful. In looking back, what kind of steps have you taken to make sure those things don't happen again?

We once had a filmmaker who was supposed to have a Q&A and she was AWOL. I went to her hotel to find her sleeping. It ended up being a really positive personal experience for her because she realized she had been burning out. She's since changed the way that she attends festivals because it was such a wake-up call. So she was incredibly apologetic.

Any kind of headaches that we have come from people who are upset and maybe feel invalidated — they take the rejection personally. I'm learning how to deal with angry, rejected filmmakers a lot better.

While we're on that subject, what's the worst thing a filmmaker's ever said to you?

I once had someone call me "small minded." It might seem inconsequential to some, but it hit me to my core. We had an email exchange in which I tried to suggest he seek out genre festivals suited to his subject matter, he called me a bunch of names until he hit me with that one. I had to write back that, "this stops here," and I stopped opening his emails.

Do you have a secret blacklist? Is he on it?

No, no, no. If somebody who's been rejected and wants to keep entering their films, I'm not going to stop them. We've had an occasional filmmaker who showed up and behaved badly — sort of like if you were at a dysfunctional family barbeque. I would be hesitant to ask him back. But on the whole, we don't really have difficult people who have attended the Festival.

You're lucky. What's the nicest thing or compliment a filmmaker has ever said to you?

I used to be flattered when filmmakers gushed that they love you so much and will always love you. But now I realize it's a lot like sex-talk, when someone says that you're the best ever — it is a genuine reaction at the time, but really is a hollow gesture.

Filmmakers say that BBFF is as good as any of the big festivals, that the program's outstanding, and all that. But we already know that. I know when they say the films are of a fantastic standard, because a lot of hard work went into making sure we're not screening anything sub-standard.

I think people generally do have a really lovely time when they're here. It's not just us trying to be open and generous, it's the fact that the Byron audience is really open, and really very, very warm towards the filmmakers. At the end of the event, there are hugs and tears, and that is very nice. But what really lasts are true friendships that start here, and blossom over time and distance. Those connections mean the most to me, and I am grateful to make and maintain them.

What are some trends that you are seeing in the most recent crop of films that have come across your desk?

That thing that I said before: filmmakers who want to be directing *CSI*, and they shoot people without needing to. It seems to me that there's a lot of unnecessary violence going on in some of the films. People should just have trust in their characters and in their scripts and not need to try and go towards a suspenseful moment that's overkill. Sometimes drama can be found from the situation without it having to be from an action.

It's also interesting watching the shift towards digital SLRs. You clearly see it in the way people are planning and shooting. They're beginning to understand the necessity for color grading a little bit more, and are using more interesting shots because the cameras are so much smaller.

Do you think that with the advances in technology, that storytelling sometimes suffers?

No, I don't think that story is suffering. I think that my programmers are suffering because it takes us longer to figure out what's good and what's not good.

Has your job jaded your opinion of film, or do you think it's expanded your appreciation?

I can say that I have learned quite a lot over the last few years. I'm now raging to get onto the film festival circuit with a film of my own, because I think I see some of the elements which make a winning combination: don't have a lingering title sequence, get to the point, keep it under thirteen minutes — or seven if you can. If you can do that, and keep your story tight and fresh, you've really got a winner right there.

If you could give would-be entrants one final piece of advice, what would it be?

Research your festivals and match your goals with their needs. Don't just throw away your money thinking, "I'm going to get into Sundance or Cannes." Research a bunch of festivals, and find the ones that are going to be the perfect fit.

Oh, and go to the Festival! This is your moment to shine, your moment to connect to the audience, to actually see how people react to your film, and how your film holds up against other films.

Finally, what three words best describe what you do?

1. Watch.
2. Feel.
3. Think.

"MEDIATE. CURATE. FACILITATE." SKY SITNEY

Former Festival Director, SILVERDOCS (now AFIDocs)

About the Festival:

- Founded in 2002, SILVERDOCS promotes documentary film as a leading art form, supports the work of independent filmmakers and fosters an atmosphere for public dialogue and civic engagement around the issues and ideas explored in the films.
- 8-day event for general audiences and industry
- Website: silverdocs.com

Sky Sitney is the Festival Director for SILVERDOCS, leading the Festival's programming, strategic development, partnerships and overall artistic vision. She joined the Festival in Fall 2005 as Director of Programming, and is recognized as one of the key contributors in helping SILVERDOCS become one of the leading festivals of its kind.

Sitney was formerly Programming Director at The Newport International Film Festival, served as the Film Programmer at the New York Underground Film Festival and is Co-Founder and Curator of the ongoing series *Fresh Film* at the Anthology Film Archives in New York City. Sitney has also held industry positions at C-Hundred Film Corp. and Fine Line Features.

In addition to her extensive programming experience, Sitney is a doctoral candidate in Cinema Studies at New York University, where she has taught film courses on a variety of genres. She is completing a dissertation on the subject of documentary film, a section of which has been recently published in the journal *Grey Room* and the book *Captured: A Lower East Side Film & Video History.*

What is the history of SILVERDOCS?

In 2002, the American Film Institute [AFI] — which at the time was sharing a space at the Kennedy Center — was invited to participate in the restoration of the beautiful, art deco Silver Theatre and to move its D.C. headquarters there. By coincidence, at the same time, Discovery Communications was moving their world headquarters just across the street. When the two realized they would be neighbors, both organizations thought that they ought to collaborate on something meaningful — combining AFI's long history of celebrating excellence in cinema with Discovery's commitment to non-fiction storytelling — the result of which was to create a documentary film festival that celebrates theatrical, high-quality non-fiction films.

How did you get involved?

This is my seventh year, so I've been here for the majority of the festival's life. I started off as the Director of Programming and then a few years ago, briefly expanded my role to Artistic Director, and ultimately took the role of Festival Director. However, I never relinquished my role as the Director of Programming when I took on these other responsibilities. While I oversee the staff and guide the overall vision of the festival, my passion for, and involvement in programming has never waned.

Prior to coming to SILVERDOCS, I was on two parallel tracks: I had already received a Masters from New York University in Cinema Studies, and was getting my PhD from the same department. I had also been curating a series at Anthology Film Archives called "Fresh Film," and was programming for the New York Underground Film Festival, and then served as the Director of Programming for the Newport International Film Festival. While at Newport, I recognized my overt interest in documentaries. Although the festival was a comprehensive one, intended to be a combination of documentary and narrative works, I couldn't quite disguise that the vast majority of my programming sensibilities seemed to be geared towards documentary. So those experiences, and a little bit of luck, gave me the opportunity to have a role at SILVERDOCS — and it's been a really compelling journey from there.

What other film festivals do you attend?

There are certain festivals that are my staples: Toronto, Sundance, IDFA [International Documentary of Amsterdam], SXSW, Tribeca, and whenever possible two lovely smaller documentary festivals: Full Frame in North Carolina and True/False in Missouri. Each year I am lucky enough to be asked to serve on the jury of some exotic festival that I have never been to, or receive invitations to a bunch of others, including events in South Africa and Mexico. I especially like the experience of attending documentary festivals that are in locations that I've never been to before, or that are playful and experimental in their approach to the form.

Do you have a favorite? What parts of these events do you admire and wish to implement at SILVERDOCS?

It's difficult to choose a favorite because each festival has its own distinct character and offers something unique. There's not one festival that embodies everything that I would wish to implement for SILVERDOCS; but perhaps there are qualities here and there that I admire or that inspire me.

For example, SXSW has the fortune of having the wonderful city of Austin as its backdrop. Its terrific film program shares the event with a major "Interactive" and "Music" festival. While this is one of the components that makes that festival so exciting, at the same time the vastness of the event can make it occasionally hard to navigate, and hard to find the filmmaking community amidst the enormous community.

I really admire the playfulness of the True/False Film Festival: they don't concern themselves with premieres, they don't place any films in a competition section — rather they present an egalitarian, very democratic, exceptionally curated film program in an intimate setting. They do wonderfully fun things, like they have a parade, host a game show — there's playfulness and an intimacy that I find very appealing.

You can't deny that Sundance has first dibs on all the most important, compelling U.S. documentaries from the year, so I covet their lineup. That doesn't mean that there are not a few "misses" amongst the numerous "hits" — but the most important documentary films of the year are likely to be screened at Sundance, and no one can argue with the excitement and buzz around the lineup that they are able to generate.

Can you describe the selection and submission process at SILVERDOCS? I send my film, what happens to it?

Even before you submit your film, there's a process already at play. We don't just sit back and hope that the great films come to us, or that films from under-represented regions find their way into our submission pool. Rather, we are highly committed to tracking and soliciting films: we do a lot of research into what films that will be ready to submit to Silverdocs. We try to attend IFP and the Good Pitch, when possible, to look at what film projects have received funding from recognized foundations, we track films in development, and work with producers to identify new content that might be a good match for us. We look carefully at the lineups of other events to see if those films are also appropriate to solicit for SILVERDOCS.

And then, of course, we receive hundreds upon hundreds, if not thousands of 'blind' submissions. We usually receive around 2,200 submissions each year to choose from.

Regardless of how the film arrives, all films go out to screeners. We have a pool of about 50 screeners, a 15-member screening committee, and three full-time staff members in programming. We always make sure that each film gets seen and reviewed by at least two screeners so that that no single person — or single sensibility — bears the full weight of determining the status of that film's trajectory in the festival.

We read the screeners reviews carefully and analyze their scores that cover everything from editing, to the quality of the cinematography and sound, to whether the film has heart, to whether the story is unique. Ultimately, the screener gives a verdict: pass, consider, or recommend.

Needless to say, we do a comparative reviewing: we make sure to look at the two screeners' scores, the two reviews that the film has received, and determine the next step. If the film has received a modest to high recommendation it goes directly to the screening committee for another look. In fact, sometimes when we see two very good film recommendations we'll even bypass the screening committee altogether and have it go directly to the senior programming staff, which is myself, our associate programmer, and our programming manager. Sometimes a film goes straight to the programming staff, such as a world premiere. We want to move quickly on these entries, because the process can literally take 6-8 weeks for a film to make its way to the top. If the score is not up to the standards of both screeners, it's usually the end of the line for that film. Occasionally we'll come across a very divisive film — a doc that one screener adores, yet another screener really dislikes — often we find these films to be the most interesting.

Throughout the programming process, we try to lock in a number of films each week so we don't find ourselves at the very end of the process having to lock in 70 features all at once. There are a lot of negotiations that may take place when we lock in a film: negotiations with distributors, broadcasters, and filmmakers who are making plans regarding their festival trajectory.

Knowing that they're in SILVERDOCS might impact or influence those plans. We also want to keep the process moving quickly because there are a number of other film festivals that literally take place during SILVERDOCS, and these filmmakers have other options. We want to make sure that they're able to attend our festival even if they have a busy calendar.

At the end of the process, there are usually about 20 open slots that we save for screening committee deliberations so that we can engage in some strategic programming. If at the end of the process we realize, "Gee! There's really not a lot of diversity in this particular lineup," or "There's not enough films on the Middle East" — or the economy, or films by women filmmakers, or whatever it is — we feel that we can do some corrective programming at that stage. Although the screening committee is weighing in all the time and filtering films up to the programmers, filling in the final 20 slots in a final deliberation meeting gives the screening committee an opportunity to be a distinct voice in shaping the final line-up.

And how long is this whole process?

The call for submissions is about six months; we typically open in mid-October and end in March. We start our screening committee meetings in December and they end in early May.

Is every film watched in its entirety?

Yes. That's actually a rule. We give our screeners and screening committee a lot of benefits. They get a full all-access pass; they can see any film at the AFI Theater year-round. We feel that the role of being a screener or on the screening committee is a job, and that job is to watch this film in its entirety. We feel when a filmmaker pays the entry fee; they are paying for the confidence of knowing that their film is going to be watched all the way until the final credit rolls off screen. Watching the entire film defines our integrity.

What qualities do you think make a good screening committee member?

I think the majority of people on a committee should have a justified, proven expertise in film. And what I mean by expertise in film is not that they, themselves, are a celebrated filmmaker — although you would love to have one or two celebrated filmmakers on the committee — but someone with a justified point of view.

We make sure we have a combination of people who have either studied film, who are critics, who have been programmers at museums or other film festivals, filmmakers, and also what I like to call a "civilian factor." These are people that are intelligent and passionate about film, but it's not necessarily their career. Our audiences are mainly civilians, and we need to be reminded of that by seeing that perspective articulated and represented on the committee. I see hundreds and hundreds of films each year, and what I consider cliché, someone else might consider very innovative. The reality factor is important.

They need to be efficient, direct, and highly articulate when writing about, and talking about how a film is working — or not working. For example, a screener might write that a film was very dull because it was wholly observational, with almost no intervention from the filmmaker. The whole thing took place in a single living room where family dynamics play out in their limited landscape. While this screener might find the observational quality a negative, someone else might see this very differently, and find the static environment critical to allowing the psychodrama to play out. So, the screener's ability to articulate clearly gave us access — a window — for someone else to intervene if they find something compelling in the description.

That said, I think, ultimately, a good screener is someone who truly has a passion and respect for film, and who can ultimately appreciate the effort made even if the film isn't a great achievement. While no single member can embody every trait, I can make sure the committee as a whole embodies it.

What are your thoughts about online screeners? Are you using them now?

We're moving in that direction bit by bit. This was not proactive on our part, but something we had to respond to. Quite frankly, we were kind of resistant at first, but now I like it for a few reasons. First, DVDs — especially home baked ones — are very unreliable. I cannot tell you how many times, once a film has been seen by a few screeners and makes its way to the committee, that committee members can't get past the first five minutes. DVDs degrade from the wear and tear that a programming committee puts them through. It is incredibly frustrating, especially when you're 45 minutes into a fantastic film, and the disc suddenly starts skipping or locking up altogether. An online submission does not have that problem.

Another good thing about online submissions is the ability to distribute a film to many screeners simultaneously. Typically, we only have two DVDs per film, so each week we have to circulate the two DVDs, and after about five weeks 10 people have seen it. But, with online screening we're able to blast it out to our screening committee members and come back the next week at our meeting and have 10 reviews. So, that's very exciting.

I'm not sure we're ready to go all-online — we are certainly not ready to weed out DVDs altogether — it took forever for us to get rid of VHS tapes — but I think we are much more comfortable now integrating online screeners into our process.

Do you guys give feedback to filmmakers?

About their score or review? Very rarely. First, with over 2,000 films submitted, we simply don't have the human resources to offer feedback to each filmmaker as to why their film wasn't accepted. Also, we announce the final lineup only weeks before the festival, and given such an intense and unforgiving schedule, we don't have time to offer detailed feedback. Even in the cases where we might want to, we literally don't have the time or manpower.

It also opens a can of worms we'd rather not deal with. Since we receive 2,000 submissions and we're only playing about a hundred films, you can imagine there are about 1,900 people that we, unfortunately, have to disappoint. That's a very painful process. I truly hate it because sometimes we have to turn down really wonderful films. Also, sometimes we get first-time filmmakers who will go on to make extraordinary works, and you don't want to be discouraging or hurt a future relationship. We might turn down a film one year, but that filmmaker might go on to make a masterpiece the following year, and you want to be in their good graces.

During the submission and review process, we do communicate with filmmakers who reach out to us to give us updates. For example, a filmmaker who just got into a festival, or won an award at a festival, or received a wonderful "Variety" review, might write, "I've been invited to/won/got great press from Festival X, but we'd rather have our world premiere at SILVERDOCS. Can you make an early decision?" There's a lot of communication that goes on in this process. Typically the communication is not so much feedback, but status updates.

And just as we cannot accept every film that is submitted, there are always a number of films that we want but we can't program for a variety of reasons. Perhaps the film will open theatrically or be broadcast nationally before our festival, or the filmmaker wants to hold out for another event — there are a million reasons why it happens, and we have to be gracious as well and think about our long-term relationships with these filmmakers, broadcasters and distributors.

I highly advise, no matter how upset or mad a filmmaker might be for not getting accepted, that one look at the submission process as an opportunity to build a long-term relationship with the programming team. Be gracious and try to understand that programming decisions are based on a variety of factors — not just whether a film is great. Filmmakers who act out, get angry or hostile, or make snide remarks disappoint us — because they're often wrong. They might claim we never watched the film, or they make other incorrect assumptions. Unfortunately, the filmmakers who are really aggressive and hostile are remembered far more than those who are very gracious. Sad, but true.

Very articulate! So, for people who tick you off, do you have a secret blacklist?

No, we don't. Although, there was one filmmaker that threatened physical harm. I told him he was not allowed to submit again. I had to wonder, "Are you going to come at me with a gun and go on a wild rampage?" It was very disturbing.

That is an understatement!

We don't need the crazy. I've had experiences where filmmakers who did not get in after repeated submissions over the years, brought the issue to my attention. "This is a festival that hasn't shown us any love," they say. So, I try to alleviate their anxiety and take the time to listen to what they have to say and to feel that they've been heard. Part of my job is about building and maintaining relationships, and quite frankly, I feel lucky that this is so. I like relationships. I'm a social person. I enjoy working with filmmakers and getting to know them. They become friends and colleagues, and I really appreciate being a part of their filmmaking journey.

But what do you do with filmmakers that are your friends, whose work you've supported for years, and for whatever reason their latest film is just not the right fit? Or they make a film we fall in love with, but for a variety of reasons, we cannot extend an invitation to. That is always difficult terrain. That's the price I have to pay — I have to be willing to be honest and forthright —and hopefully do it in a gracious way that allows the relationship to be maintained.

So, what are some of the reasons great films don't make it into festivals?

There are a variety of factors. First of all, as I mentioned earlier, in addition to the films that are already being submitted for consideration, we solicit films from other festival lineups. We keep an eye on how many films we're programming from Sundance or Toronto or SXSW. We program a robust number of films from these events each year at the festival, but we don't want to replicate their entire program. We want our slate to be balanced, and we know that many of our audience members already saw the Grand Jury Prize from Sundance at another venue.

Another factor involves the themes that have already been represented by other works. For example, there might be a wonderful film on clean water in India, and a second film comes along that's just as wonderful. On occasion we will have more than one film on a similar subject, but can you have three films? Can you have four? There's a point where you're not expanding the dialogue with the audience, but regurgitating the same subject matter.

Also, a film might literally open two days after its festival screening at a local commercial theater. That's when I have to say, "Look, this is a wonderful doc, but what real service will SILVERDOCS be giving the film?" Yes, it will help the local success of the film, but you don't want to do that too much because then how are you using the festival in the service of some films and not others? When we have over 2,000 films submitted, I recognize and respect that there is a lot that we can do for our films, and if we're giving all the spots to films that already have a following, or, already have played a major festival circuit, or already have a major distributor behind them, we're not really leveraging the festival for the some of the filmmakers who could seriously benefit from it.

There are just so many different factors — these are just some of the ones off the top of my head. I'm sure that there's more that I could think of.

I think those cover a great deal of ground.
What are your thoughts about premiere status? How important is it at SILVERDOCS?

It's a balance. We're certainly not an exclusively premiere-oriented festival, as the majority of the films at SILVERDOCS are not premieres. That said they do have to be DC premieres. But each year we do launch a hearty number of films. This year we had 14 premieres (World, North American, and US, combined). Because SILVERDOCS also holds a concurrent five-day conference of workshops, panels, and pitching forums, we attract a lot of industry people. They have already been to Sundance and SXSW, and we need to provide them with new material to make their time here exciting and productive.

At the same time, we know where we stand. If a filmmaker has an opportunity to launch at Sundance, they're not likely to turn it down to come to SILVERDOCS — we understand our position in the festival universe and don't apologize for it or try to pretend that we're something we're not. Rather, we celebrate what we are. At the end of the day, I want to know that the festival is proud to screen each film. I don't want to put premiere status over quality.

We end up showing some wonderful films that you're likely to see nominated for the Academy Awards, or that won the Critic's Choice Award. And while we proactively search for the hot titles from other major festivals, we also do a lot to try and find those gems that will be the next big film. Whether a film is a world premiere, or just something that's a little bit under the radar, there's a balance that seems to work for us — that fits in with where we are as a festival, and what we can do best.

Are you influenced by big names attached to films? For a documentary, that would most likely mean a famous director or producer.

Part of our goal is to present the current season of stellar documentary films to our audiences. And, no doubt, if Michael Moore makes a film, it's probably going to be an important film in that year's documentary landscape, and we would like to play a part in it. But if you look at our history, we have shown relatively few Michael Moore films. It is not for lack of interest, but more a reflection of how the market works. Moore's films — and other documentaries like it that are represented by major distributors — tend to go from their premieres at such festivals as Cannes, Toronto, or Sundance directly into theaters, and don't tend to do an extensive film festival run.

So, we're influenced by so-called "big names" in the sense that we are aware of the work, and when possible we would like to include that work in our slate alongside the other filmmakers' perspectives that we value, such as the first-time filmmaker or filmmaker from an under-represented region.

How important is the audience in your final selection process?

We feel that our role is not to program for the already existing sensibilities of our audience, but to program for our idealized audience. We don't want to dumb down, or assume that a particular film might be too challenging for our audience — it's actually the opposite. We want to create a line up that encourages the audience to continue to evolve and grow and to be able to explore documentaries that are pushing boundaries.

Now, we're not going to program a full lineup of cutting edge, provocative films, but we do choose a few films each year that we expect will challenge our viewers. I love programming films that might be a little unconventional, or might be a little perplexing or uncomfortable to watch. We might put them in our smallest theater of 75 seats, knowing that it will draw a very small but hopefully appreciative audience.

It's very rare to find a light hearted, happy, funny documentary. We very rarely come across documentaries that are family friendly. So last year we screened *Being Elmo*, which is not only family friendly, but it also happens to be a wonderful documentary. It was the kind of film that people could bring their young kids to see. Elmo himself was here, embodied by his charming creator Kevin Clash, and the audience just ate it up. So, audience is important in terms of knowing whom you're serving.

I had a brief stint once serving as a programmer for the New York Underground Film Festival. There are certain films that I come across that, if I were still programming for that festival, would be a slam-dunk, but it truly won't work in the context of a documentary festival. You do need to know what fits. Does that answer the question?

Beautifully. And it's a very different take than many festivals, so it's important. A lot of festivals program for an existing audience, and I don't fault them for that because, ultimately, they have to sell tickets. But their market is different than yours, which is heavily influenced by the attendance of industry professionals.

What's the role of distributors in your process? I know that some doc films already come to festivals with a distribution deal in place.

I would say that about a third of the films we show already have a distributor attached by the time the film screens here. Sometimes we'll have to negotiate with a distributor rather than the filmmaker to get their film here. Luckily, we have really great relationships with many distributors with whom we communicate regularly — they will let us know what they have in their pipeline, and we will reach out to them with what selections interest us. With a few distributors, we have to make a bigger case for why their film would work here, and we don't always win that battle. For every film that plays SILVERDOCS, there's always one that got away. No one knows at the end of the day when the line-up is announced which ones we didn't have, but we do lose some battles with distributors.

We also have similar relations with sales agents, executive producers with a proven body of work, cultural institutions, and even embassies, who make us aware of works that are relevant from the region that they represent. It's just one more part of the complex infrastructure that we're working with.

And you have to understand that each distributor has a different goal. Some don't want any press attention or are concerned that a festival screening might take away from the audience when the film is theatrically released, and thus they want us to program the film in the smallest possible theater. Others may want opening night, and no screening can be more high profile or large enough. So understanding what the distributor wants is imperative. They have different strategies for different titles. It's all part of what keeps the job interesting. Programming is a jigsaw puzzle in which the pieces change daily.

Do you allow your sponsors or donors any influence in the programming process?

Gratefully, no. We defined our relationship with our original founding sponsor, Discovery Communications, from the get-go. Discovery is clearly in the business of content, but they've been very respectful, and highly protective of the boundaries of the festival program.

I know that in order for us to maintain our success and reputation, we cannot compromise on the quality of the program. We can't be seen as losing our integrity, and I don't want to do a bait and switch on our audiences. That is, we've cultivated a really amazing audience who put their trust in us. And I don't want to subject someone who's counting on us, and is willing to take a chance on us, and stand in line for an hour and a half to go see a film, to have to encounter a film that's only programmed because the sponsor wants it. I make it very clear that our audience cannot be bought or sold. And at the end of the day, it has made us more coveted by sponsors, not less. Because the program is good.

Occasionally we will create a thematic strand such as films dealing with peace building and conflict resolution or global health. In such cases we will work with specific partners to highlight certain films that address such issues. Typically, we work with sponsors whose mission matches the festival — and the films that we select for that particular thematic strand, and as a result the sponsor enhances an experience at SILVERDOCS that was always already put in place, and does not just create a new experience that we must cater to.

Excellent. What elements do you think add up to make a successful film?

That's a good question. First, a clear, confident, aesthetic point of view is key. There are so many different kinds of documentaries: polemical and advocacy-oriented; experimental and artistic; personal quests; personal dramas; biopics. And there are so many different styles that a film can successfully embody.

How do you compare a traditionally structured, historical doc like *Eyes on the Prize* to something like *October Country*, which is more lyrical? What do they have in common? I think it's a sense that how the film is presented is not by accident, not by some sheer luck, but by assured, proactive, decision making. The film is articulated by someone using a distinct film language that they're well versed in.

I also think curiosity — a filmmaker who approaches a film with a question rather than an answer makes a better film. It allows the filmmaker to keep the film moving in unanticipated directions. In such cases the filmmaker does not necessarily set out to make a film where they know where it's going to end up, but allows the filmmaking itself to become a journey —where in the end both the audience and the filmmaker learn something new. I think that is a much more honest style of documentary filmmaking.

Ultimately, the choice to tell a story through film rather than any other art form, such as the written word or song or performance is deliberate and important. So I ask, "Why and how must this story be told through the medium of film? How does the filmmaker take advantage of filmmaking media to tell it?" Occasionally, I'll see a film and think it would've been better as a New Yorker article. And of course other times, you'll see films and can't imagine it being told any other way because the filmmaker did such a good job using the strengths of this medium.

That was very eloquent. Thank you.
Is any topic taboo at SILVERDOCS?

Interesting. A couple of years ago, we came across a film that was essentially pornographic; extremely artistic (and somewhat disturbing) pornography that wasn't so much titillating as it was fascinating. I knew a couple of other festivals that played it, but I didn't feel comfortable. This goes with what I said before about the audience: I want to program films that are pushing the boundaries, but this particular film pushed the boundaries in a manner that we didn't feel was appropriate for who we are and who our audience is.

I think if I came across a film that was in-and-of itself racist or sexist or generally offensive, then I might feel the perspective of the filmmaker really didn't deserve a platform, and there was nothing to learn from it, I would see that as a red flag — even if the film is well made. There are just films out there that have no moral or social value. That's not to say that we're not interested in showing films dealing with racism, or homophobia, or sexism, but I don't need or desire to screen a film that is, in itself, racist, homophobic or sexist. So I think we would draw the line there.
As you can imagine, I often hear that documentary festivals, ours included, have a liberal bias. Part of that is inherent in the documentary genre: It is an art form typically embraced by people with a more liberal mindset. The films that come across my desk rarely if ever represent a strong Conservative, Christian or Tea Party perspective. If there was a very strong film made from that perspective, I cannot say we wouldn't show it. We literally do not get a lot of those films.

That makes perfect sense to me. Do you have a favorite success story?

A particular story doesn't come to mind, but I do know that filmmakers who have won an award at SILVERDOCS are often surprised by the avalanche of invitations that follow from other high profile festivals. In some cases, awards from Silverdocs can also lead to a distribution or broadcast or VOD [video on demand] deal.

I also hear of people who meet future collaborators here, or learn about a new story while here. While at SILVERDOCS a few years ago, Canadian filmmaker Patrick Reed, who was here with a film called *Triage: Dr. James Orbinski's Humanitarian Dilemma* learned about a Kenyan soap opera about a soccer team whose storyline combined AIDS, condom use, and trying to overcome racial differences. He found it so fascinating that he ended up making the documentary film, *The Team* about it.

And of course, I am always happy when people can make connections with other industry people, distributors, broadcasters, and festival programmers

— and create real relationships with other filmmakers.

What's the nicest thing a filmmaker has ever said to you?

At the end of the festival, there's always a flood of beautiful, warm, kind remarks. Sometimes people have said that they can see our "total vision." I laugh because I don't know what the program looks like before we start programming, and if a total vision develops, it does so organically.

One question I get all the time is, "So what is the theme for the festival this year?" I don't ever sit in my little office and decide what the theme of the program is going to be, because I don't believe in setting a programmatic agenda and then looking for films that fit that agenda. Rather, I like to be responsive to the themes that naturally emerge out of the work itself. It is not appropriate or fair for me to approach the 2,000-plus film submissions with an ulterior motive; I need to go out there with a clean mental slate, look at what the films are on their own terms, and be open and responsive to the collective unconscious out there.

So, I appreciate that people say that there is a total vision — and in a way there is. What I believe or hope they mean by that there is a sense that the program is not haphazard, but rather there's something cohesive about it. Not all the films are in dialogue with each other, but there's an overarching cohesiveness amongst the films.

I agree that in any year, there is a zeitgeist — a spirit of the times — that forms a unique mood among filmmakers. Which brings me to ask, are you seeing any thematic or artistic or even technical trends in the films you've been watching recently?

Thankfully, the worst of the trends, which of course we call clichés, don't make their way up to me. I'm buffered from these films by the screeners or the committee and programming staff. The kinds of trends I'm talking about here are oriented towards production styles; things like slick crane shots swooping down on favelas, or shantytowns – something we've come to call "poverty porn." Then there are trends in terms of topics. One trend that has not yet slowed down is the slam poetry, hip-hop film — and from every country you can imagine. And for whatever reason, last year we received a lot of films on coal mining, or mining in general. It's amazing. And this year, we received three films about bestiality. Who knew?!

These are very specific. In more general terms, documentaries about a personal or a family member with a health issue, where the filmmaker takes a personal journey as they deal with the crisis. Sometimes this can work very successfully and can be brilliant, but often it ends up as self-indulgent or narcissistic in a way that doesn't translate to an outsider. We see a lot of that.

There's a lot of creative license being taken these days in documentary filmmaking that we find exciting. I feel that documentarians today see themselves more as creative interpretations of reality, rather than strict observers. So, rather than being strict observers, filmmakers have become creative re-interpreters. This allows a bit more leeway to play with animation or re-enactments, which have made a comeback.

I feel like filmmakers are less burdened today than they might have been a couple decades ago about their having to reveal the full truth, and wondering how much their own choices influenced that. Now, there's so much more flexibility in how a filmmaker conveys truth. I think we are at a point where everyone agrees you really can't ever convey full truth, so let's not strive so hard in that direction. Filmmakers are allowed and encouraged to play around with their interpretation of truth. Of course, this can get dangerous, because audiences essentially believe that what they're seeing is complete and unbiased truth. That is when you may run into some problems.

There are, of course, still filmmakers working in very unmediated styles. They are still committed to direct cinema in a beautiful and wonderful way. But at the same time there are a lot of filmmakers out there integrating the techniques more associated with narrative storytelling than documentary film.

I often feel that documentary filmmakers are able to really be creative — more so than narrative filmmakers. While all films need to follow the tradition of the story arc, narrative filmmakers better stay on course over that hill, or the audience will not follow. Documentarians can veer more off course, as long as the windy ride ultimately follows along the path.

Has your job jaded your opinion on film, or opened your appreciation towards it?

I don't think I have been jaded, because I'm literally, right in the moment, immersed in my own screening. And I still get that thrill and excitement when I see a great film. I still feel that joy upon seeing a wonderful film. However, I think that my relationship to film has changed. My job is very challenging and my role at SILVERDOCS has evolved, so in addition to programming I am now involved with fundraising, administrative logistics, and management. It has made me appreciate and respect my role as a programmer even more.

I'm very grateful and lucky to have found the thing I love, because, after all these years, I still find the pleasure in it. That's not to say I find the pleasure in watching bad films, I certainly don't, but I know that you have to go through the bad to get to the gems — and the gems are all the more meaningful and exciting because of the comparison.

Finally, what three words best describe what you do?

Mediate, curate, facilitate.

"DEVELOP MEANINGFUL RELATIONSHIPS" JOANNE FEINBERG

Former Director of Programming, Ashland Independent Film Festival

About the Festival:

- Founded in 2001, the Ashland Independent Film festival celebrates the diversity of human experience through the art of independent film — enriching, educating and inspiring audiences of all ages.
- 5-day regional event for general audiences
- Website: ashlandfilm.org

A graduate of the prestigious Tisch School of the Arts at New York University with a B.F.A. in Cinema Studies and Film Production, Joanne Feinberg knew from age nine, fiddling with a 35 mm camera, that her future would involve film. Before relocating to Ashland, Oregon, Joanne worked for 15 years editing and producing various award-winning documentaries in New York and San Francisco.

Joanne is now in her eighth year as the Director of Programming for the Ashland Independent Film Festival. Attendees have come to expect great things from the Festival, held downtown in the historic art-deco Varsity Theatre, where excellent programming and interactions with filmmakers are the norm in a close-knit community that features 80 films in five days.

Joanne, you know that my affinity for Ashland (AIFF) is no secret. As a filmmaker at the first year of the event, I have followed the event closely – and make it a regular stop on my festival circuit. What is the Festival's history, and when did you become involved with it?

The inaugural festival was in 2001. I got involved as a volunteer screener in 2003 for the 2004 festival, and from there was asked to become a member of the Board. At that time the Festival was very small and they didn't have a programming department per se. I was asked to help with the programming of the Festival, which was being done by the Executive Director and Managing

Director. I resigned from my Board role and began to create the role of Lead Programmer which developed into my current role as Director of Programming. It was an organic process, discovering what was needed and how it would grow.

Your background is in film. Were you working in the industry before you came to the Festival?

Yes, I went to film school at NYU and worked in production in New York City for two years before I went to San Francisco, where I worked as a freelance editor of documentaries, corporate films and commercials. I did that type of work for 15 years before I came to Ashland.

Did you work with any other festivals before Ashland, or was this your first?

My first job in college was as the assistant to the Programmer of the Bleecker Street Cinema. This was in the days before Netflix, and they screened two or more classic, "independent," and "foreign" films every day of the year. Watching these films on the big screen was a great supplement to my degree in Cinema Studies! I was also a juror for festivals in the Bay Area. I had experience in that aspect of programming, and I attended many festivals including the San Francisco International Film Festival, which I considered to be my source of continuing education in the film world.

How many festivals do you get to attend now?

It varies year to year. I try to attend at least five, but it depends on our budget and time constraints. Attending other events is an integral part of the job for me, not only to see new films, but also to network with filmmakers and in the industry and build new relationships. Seeing new work on the big screen with audiences is very helpful, too.

Which would you say is your favorite festival, and why has it served as a model for Ashland?

I have been to a number around the world and really love IDFA in Amsterdam and the Toronto International Film Festival for many reasons, but I would say Sundance is still an outstanding experience for me every year.

I think the gathering of so many filmmakers at one place at one time is very invigorating for me. It is my model of excellence in running a film festival. And of course, the timing is perfect for us to scout new films to screen in April.

And it shows through your programming and speakers. Can you describe the submission and acceptance process? I make a film and send you the disk — now what happens?

Our call for entries starts each year on September 1. At that point, we open our doors in many ways: putting out a general call for entries on our website, Facebook, blogs, our selected email lists, and also through Withoutabox.com, which is the primary source of our entries.

Our website has very extensive information about submitting entries. It is constantly updated, and tells you about the kind of films our festival shows, who has won our awards, who our jurors are, quotes from filmmakers who have attended — so filmmakers can get a feel for who we are as a festival. I hope filmmakers do their homework to decide if their film is a good fit with our festival. Although, with that said, we are open to seeing all kinds of new, quality work and do not have prescribed limits to the kind of submissions we will consider.

Once we receive a film, it goes through a screening process that has been refined over the years. When I started in 2004, there were close to 100 local volunteer film screeners, but over the years, we have pared down our screeners to twenty. It is a volunteer position, but we ask prospective screeners to complete an application process where they screen and write reviews of films. Many in the group of twenty have been doing this for five or six years. It is a huge time commitment — some of our screeners put in over 80 to 100 hours in just over two months. They take their job very seriously.

Our mantra is that we treat each submission that comes in to our festival with great respect. Every film is screened by at least two people, and sometimes even five, six, or seven, including all of our programmers. At least two screeners must watch the film in its entirety. They then write in-depth reviews of the films — not necessarily long write-ups and synopses, but we ask for an evaluation that considers many different aspects of the film. The reviews are submitted directly to me and I read them all. From there, a decision will be made as to where the film will go: some will be seen twice by our screeners and it's determined that the film is not suitable for the Festival; others continue up through the process. A film that passes the first set of screeners then goes through the second round, and then goes to me, or my team of programmers. This year there were three on that team.

Out of the 837 films you received last year, how many get to your desk?

I see many, many films each year, because I like to get a good feel for the range of submissions we are receiving. Even if a movie was viewed by two or more screeners and I know it won't go further in the process, I might still watch a film because there is some element that warrants my attention. Either myself or another programmer will see all the films submitted by our alumni. And of course, I also see additional films at other festivals.

What changes to your system would you like to make in the future or do you think it is working pretty well for you?

I think it is working really well. There is always the concern you will miss that "one outstanding film" if you don't personally watch every film, but we feel that the films that are best for Ashland rise up through the process, and that all the films are treated with a lot of respect by our screeners. I have great trust in our system.

Do you charge a submission fee? What is the justification for doing so?

We do, and we discuss this in depth every year. But the truth is, it's quite costly to us to process all the entries that come in, track them, screen them as extensively as we do, and manage our volunteers in a way that we feel honors the films. We could not do it without charging an entry fee — it just covers our administrative costs.

What are your feelings on fee waivers?

We waive the fees for all AIFF Alumni. And I do extend waivers in very specific circumstances. The truth is there are certain films we wouldn't get to see if we did not waive the fee.

Do you give feedback to filmmakers?

Only if asked, and only after the letters of acceptance or rejection go out. Otherwise no. It is not an easy process to do so, and by the time our letters are sent out, we are busy with other programming and logistical issues.

Do you find media kits useful in making decisions?

Rarely. My staff and I are not influenced by pretty media kits. We might refer to the kit to see certain information such as where the film has played before. We really only look at the online information that comes through our internal system or Withoutabox.

What is the biggest mistake a filmmaker can make when submitting a film to you?

While this does not happen often, when someone submits an early bird application and misses sending the film in by the deadline, it causes extra work for our staff to follow-up. Our early entry fee is heavily discounted on the assumption that those filmmakers should be able to get their materials to us on time.

Do you pay screening fees?

Screening fees are a luxury we can rarely afford. They are usually reserved for the films of our special guests for which we must go through a distributor.

What type of hospitality does AIFF extend to filmmakers?

We pride ourselves on our hospitality! Our filmmaker liaisons are extraordinary and oversee every detail of ensuring that our filmmakers are very well taken care of! A volunteer picks up all filmmakers at the airport and takes them to complimentary accommodations. We give VIP passes for all screenings, parties and other special events. We have nightly happy hours, and our hospitality suite provides snack and drinks. We have received grants in the past from the Academy of Motion Picture Arts and Sciences and this year from the National Endowment for the Arts to help offset some filmmaker travel.

I have to interject: the hospitality at AIFF was an eye-opener for me. When I played the Festival in 2001, I was at the end of a year-long circuit, and had been to about thirty festivals. AIFF was the only one who literally held my hand from the moment my plane landed to the time I left. I ate meals with other filmmakers, stayed at the home of a film enthusiast, and forged life-long friendships because of the opportunities for everyone to mingle. It is still a model for many other events to emulate.

And, Jon, the long and wonderful relationship that has continued with you over the years is what we strive for!

What are the panel discussions like at AIFF?

We offer free filmmaker "TALKback" forums geared to general audiences. It is an opportunity for our audience to have additional interaction with the filmmakers — they love this aspect of the Festival. We present a variety of panels each year, for short films, features and documentaries, on topics that organically emerge from the films selected that year. They are all moderated by our wonderful industry guests to keep the discussion focused. And they always run over — no one wants the conversation to stop!

What are some of the esthetics of films you like to program for Ashland?

First, we are very lucky to have an open-minded audience, and want to offer them a diverse sample of what we think is out there. They are often willing to take a chance, and they trust us. We program for our overall audience, but do keep the demographics in mind, which is skewed older and wealthier, but also engaged, artistic, intelligent and with the ability to like many types of film.

We have had years of "heavy" docs, and people have commented that we show only dark and depressing films — but of course those are the very ones that sell best each year!

People want to know what is happening out there in the world and want to be challenged and want to think about the issues of the day. I think we are very fortunate.

Are there any red flags or taboo topics you cannot show?

No. We don't have a midnight screening which affords an option to broaden the type of programming we can show. It is my hope that sometime in the future we will have one, but not at the moment.

The first year, there was a midnight show, because that is the time slot I played. It sold out! And my film was, at the time, considered racy. But I also think the Festival was trying to figure out what they were about — as all good events do. AIFF ended up less sexy — but much more thought-provoking.

I think both have their place!

What are your thoughts about premiere status?

We don't require it, and don't expect to in the future. Submissions must be no older than two years, and most of our films are produced within the last year to eighteen months. We do not discriminate because a film has been shown somewhere else first. While worldly, our community does not have the chance to see many of these films anywhere else, so to discriminate on the basis of a previous screening doesn't benefit us or the filmmaker.

When making decisions on films, are you influenced by what awards a film has won elsewhere?

No, although I do look at that on their entry form, and that fact might pique my interest. Sometimes, I will see many awards listed from festivals I have never heard of, and that can be a red flag.

Are you influenced by big names — stars or directors — associated with a film?

No. It is rare that there are big names attached to the films we screen. However, I do think our audiences like to have that name recognition occasionally. What makes me happy is when they seek out the work of our alumni filmmakers who are not big stars or directors, but because we have grown to become fans of their films after seeing and meeting them in Ashland!

If two submissions were exactly equal in quality and storytelling, would you prefer to take the one with the big name?

Maybe.

Have you ever programmed a film that you thought was fabulous and the audience did not like it?

It happens with a film or two every year. But it is part of the process and I wouldn't expect it to be any different, nor would I do it any differently! Overall, our audience has stated that the quality of films they see has increased every year, and their trust in us as curators has grown as well.

Are you ever influenced by donors or sponsors to program a film?

No. We have had some incredibly hard conversations over whether films should get in for many different reasons — someone knows somebody or it is an alumni film. In the end, we do what is best for the Festival.

What role do distributors play in your programming?

None, really. We have found that because of our regional size, distributors want fees and we normally don't pay them. Sometimes a distributor will know we want a specific film and they will work with us. But we have never – and will not — program a film at the insistence of a distributor.

Okay, so you have reviewed 800+ films and have a list of potential finalists. How do you plan your schedule? How do you put it all together?

We have an unusual situation with a wide range of theaters that seat from 30 to 550. We develop a grid for each day and time slot, and try to find the balance between film appeal, theater capacity, time of screening, conflicts with concurrent programming, and ultimately, what is right for the film.

There are some personal films we feel would get lost in a big theater, and there are some films that are naturally meant to be in large theaters with big sound. We also play films in small theaters multiple times — sometimes every day of the Festival. Even though they are in a small venue, we want to give our filmmakers access to the audience as much as possible. Some of our best Q&As are in our smaller theaters, because the conversations there are so intimate.

When putting the grid together, do you ever have to jettison a film because there just aren't enough slots?

Sadly yes. Sometimes, when we are notifying the filmmakers that they are in or not, we may tell a filmmaker that we can't fit that film in, and we will hold it for a week or two to see if we can somehow make it work. One year, we could not fit a film in, but programmed it for the following year. Other times, we have been able to fit them in that year when another films drop out although it is rare.

Do you curate from other festivals?

Yes. I definitely choose films from my trip to Sundance and some of the other Fall festivals that we attend.

How important is your relationship with other film festival directors?

It is so important. I see many of them at other festivals. It is a great way to share information. There are many other festivals at the same time as ours, so we are often in communication about programming the same film and getting the filmmaker to both festivals. These relationships have strengthened over the years.

I don't often talk with other directors about films they are showing, but that is something I can see trying to do in the future. I would like to develop more cooperative working relationships with some of these festival directors, but it is often hard to make the time to develop these relationships. I am hoping the new "Festival Forum" program through IFP (Independent Filmmaker Project) will benefit festivals and filmmakers.

What is more important — schooling or storytelling?

Storytelling rules in all cases!

What industry publications or websites do you read, and do they influence you at all?

I read *IndieWire, Filmmaker Magazine*, and browse about thirty other blogs by different writers and filmmakers every day. I feel they are a great source of information. It keeps me current, and gives insight to the filmmakers' mind-set, their experience in making the film, and the festival circuit. And I must admit, Facebook and twitter are invaluable.

Do you have a favorite success story of a film that has played at AIFF?

There is the story of *Wild Parrots of Telegraph Hill* which went on to be a great success. Judy has been quoted as saying, "We applied to all the big festivals and were turned down by everyone — and then came to Ashland — and won an award and went on to become one of the highest grossing docs at that time." She found the perfect audience here, and that audience helped make her success.

What is the nicest thing a filmmaker has ever told you?

Just recently, Adam Reid was on the red carpet at the Indie Spirit Awards and spoke about Ashland, how much he loved our festival and our audiences, and he actually called it "filmmaker heaven." He put it in the context of going to some big city festivals, but regional festivals were the best experiences he ever had. To me, that was the best praise, because it is all about the filmmakers and connecting them to audiences and having a great experience. Hearing that makes me feel really good.

What is the worst thing a filmmaker has ever told you?

I guess I have selective amnesia, because I can't think of examples for the bad things.

Ha ha! Do you get angry calls from filmmakers when you reject them?

I write personal "rejection" letters to as many filmmakers as possible — literally hundreds each year. I find that it really helps filmmakers to hear from me directly. It is so painful — there are a lot of films I do love, but can't put in the Festival.

And by keeping the lines of communication open, I have made a lot of friends. I have rejected people four or five times in a row and then gone on to program their film. They have come to Ashland, had a great experience, and we have become good friends. It's just part of the whole process.

In general, angry comments have lessened quite a bit over the years. We have a strong mission to respond to any upset filmmaker on the day we hear from them. When they hear back in a timely and respectful manner, it lessens the tension. That has been important to me.

Do you have a secret blacklist?

No, I don't.

If you heard someone was difficult at another festival, would that influence you as to whether you would take their film?

No, absolutely not. Honestly, I have heard that about some filmmakers, then had them attend, and we have had a great time. Sometimes it is a perception. These films are their babies, and they are very protective.

You go into the situation knowing how much these films mean to them, and the difficulties cease to exist. Even with the rare projection issue that arises for example, once these are resolved and the lights come up and Q&A starts, the audience is happy and the filmmaker interacts well — these situations resolve themselves.

With the films coming across your desk this year, what technology, storytelling or thematic trends do you see?

This year, I have observed filmmakers taking on some very serious global and national issues on an epic scale — which is reflective of what is happening in our world today. At the same time, there are many very intimate and personal stories. Occasionally, they meet in the middle, and combine both. Those are always winners.

The trend of competition-based films persists, and that is getting tiresome except in some very rare cases!

Do you see the impact of technology on the films you are receiving?

Only improving them. I think the trend of shooting films on iPhones is intriguing, but not there yet. We did have a few of those that were not included in the Festival for various reasons.

Do you think that new technology adds to the storytelling or do you think people are just using technology because it is cool?

I think some filmmakers have mastered technology but not storytelling. And it all comes back to storytelling. But some have mastered both — and those are the films I am looking for…

Is the recent proliferation of lots of film schools helping or hindering the submissions you are receiving?

I am seeing a lot of great work from many film schools, big and small. I think Stanford's documentary program is outstanding. There are some really strong filmmakers coming out of film school — I don't discredit it.

When someone comes to Ashland for the Festival, what should they do to get the most out of their experience?

I would tell filmmakers not to miss their Q&A sessions, and attend as many films and parties as possible. They each receive a VIP pass, and should use it to take advantage of all the Festival offers. And enjoy the beauty of Oregon — go for a hike in Lithia Park and the surrounding areas.

Do you think your experience as a programmer has jaded or expanded your appreciation of film?

It has totally expanded my appreciation of independent films — and made me less tolerant of Hollywood studio films, which I think have less heart.

If you could give an entrant one piece of advice, what would it be?

Wait until your film is really ready to show us. If you have elements that are not ready, don't submit for the early deadline, but wait until the later deadline to submit a really complete film. We do see rough cuts, and we can view works in progress — but a film must have its basic structure in place before it is ready to go to festivals.

Agreed. Don't rush just to play a festival. There is always next year. What three words best describe what you do?

Develop meaningful relationships.

"LOOK. WORRY. INTERACT." HELEN STEPHENSON

Festival Founder and Director, Prescott Film Festival (Arizona)

About the Festival:

- Supports independent films and filmmakers by featuring them through the festival and special screenings, while enhancing the cultural and economic welfare of the quad-city area (Prescott Valley, Chino Valley, Dewey-Humboldt, and Prescott) and returning the region to its filmmaking roots, which began in 1912.
- 8-day event for general audiences targeting local film enthusiasts, Phoenix, Flagstaff, and parts of Southern California.
- Web: prescottfilmfestival.com

Helen Stephenson is one of the new breeds of festival directors — a frustrated filmmaker who believed that there had to be a better way to run a festival, and that her community needed to connect through the medium of film. So she created one from scratch.

Before she started the Prescott Film Festival, Helen worked as freelance writer/producer for more than two decades. After attending the California State University at Long Beach and working at KTTV Los Angeles, she started her own production company which produced documentaries, and has written and co-produced twelve feature films.

Helen, let's start with how you started the Prescott Film Festival.

I was walking downtown with a friend and she said she thought it would be a perfect place for a film festival and I agreed. The town has a population of around 30,000 people. Add that to the population of the rest of our Central Arizona Highlands and all together there's 100,000 or so close by, so we put our heads together to think about it. My friend wanted to be a filmmaker, and my degree and background was in film. I had lived in California as a filmmaker, and the idea seemed like something that could happen really easily — yeah, right! — even though I knew that there had been two or three attempts to have a film festival in Prescott, and all of them had failed. So my friend and I decided that we were going to bring a film festival to Prescott. We started researching other festivals in January 2009 and went to the Sedona International Film Festival that year. Putting on our own festival was topmost in our minds. We asked lots of questions from volunteers and staff at the Festival. We then chose a feature, short, and guest filmmaker from their festival and started a "Monthly Series" in May 2009. Eventually my friend decided she wanted to go to film school and dropped out of the Festival before the first annual event took place in 2010. So the number of hours devoted to putting the Festival together really grew exponentially!

We developed the Festival's mission, and I think that we have done a good job of meeting our main goals of bringing together filmmakers and audiences.

You said your background was in film – tell us more about that.

I majored in film and graduated from Cal State Long Beach with a Bachelor's Degree and dabbled in game shows and TV newsrooms for a time, since I thought I wanted to work in television. Then I started to create and produce training and product demonstration films for various companies. Through that experience, I decided to form a production company with my then husband to make straight-to-video movies. I ended up writing fourteen scripts, of which twelve were produced.

Had you worked at other festivals before creating PFF?

I hadn't worked at any festivals, but I did cover a few as an arts and entertainment reporter for *Prescott eNews*, a local online newspaper. Among the events I attended was the Sedona Film Festival; I was basically a regular there, attending off and on almost from the beginning. So I started writing detailed articles about the event. I became friendly with their executive director, Patrick Sweiss, and he started to mentor us. That connection was instrumental in getting us launched. Their "do this" or "don't do that" advice and honest and in-depth insight was key. Whatever we asked, they answered. Without their help, we could not have done it.

Did you attend other film festivals before your created PFF?

I had attended many festivals as a filmmaker. Our production company would sell the U.S. distribution rights to make our production budget, and we would keep the foreign rights. So we would trek to MIFED [market in Milan, Italy],

AFM [American Film Market in Santa Monica, CA] and Cannes, but we would attend these as sellers, not audience members.

How many festivals do you get to now?

One — mine. I'm kidding! I also attend Phoenix Film Festival, which has also been incredibly supportive as we started PFF. And of course, the Sedona Film Festival. They both put on a fabulous festival and treat the filmmakers like gold. I believe that is what you should be doing, because otherwise, you would not have a festival.

I want to talk to you about your submission and selection process. Can you describe how that works at PFF?

Like most events, it starts with our application form on the website. We do not use an online service, but have a form that needs to be downloaded and sent back to us. But we have no advertising budget — whatever I needed to spend came out of pocket — and although I put the call for entries out on various websites, only about twenty percent of our submissions come through this way.

However, since we are still just getting started, I research other festival websites and I see what happened at their events — which films were selected, which films won what awards, and then I watch all the trailers. I like to refer to it as "festival mining." For these films, I send letters and will waive their submission fees — whatever I need to do to get the filmmaker interested, because we are just starting out. I probably spend close to twelve hours a day researching films, and probably for about four months or so until I have enough selections for my programmers to watch.

The films are all sent to our office and I take the first look at the entries. If I know that it will not play to the audiences in Prescott, or will be offensive to our programmers, it dies right there. Recently, I had an entry that started out with blood spurting out every place. Horror doesn't play in Prescott. Even if it is the most fabulous film on the planet, we can't do it. Our audiences would walk out. Or worse, never return.

So if I think it is something that will play — whether I personally like it or not, and I work diligently to keep my politics out of it — the film is sent on to our programmers.

We have thirty programmers. They will come by the office and pick up the

DVD and scoring form and watch at home. This goes on for about four or five months. Afterwards, the scores are added up, and the top films in each category are sent to a second "official selection" jury who watch all of the films. This committee is made up of the programmers who have watched a majority of the films already. If a programmer only watched three of the movies, they won't make the cut to be on the jury. This select group meets and discusses all of the entries and decides the Jury Award Winners.

I do not vote in this discussion, but I will provide behind-the-scenes information. If they are vacillating on a film, or cannot choose between two movies, I ask if they want the behind-the-scene story and if so, share any background of the film's production I may know with them. For instance, last year we offered a "Best Emerging Filmmaker" award for a first film. There were two films that were really, really close to winning, but the jury couldn't decide. I told them that one director created the entire film on his own, and the other had hired a locally well-known, professional editor. The jury presented the award to the one-man show.

How many of your programmers or screeners are "film professionals?"

One person out of the thirty.

I am amazed that everything is done on paper. So you say that twenty percent are blind submissions and the other eighty percent are curated or researched?

Yes. We haven't moved into the paperless office yet. Part of that is because our programmers are older, and not tech-savvy. Many of them still have dial-up so there's no way they can watch a film online. Last year I had an online submission and only about three of the programmers had the ability to watch it.

Do you charge a submission fee? Why?

We only charge the fee to the twenty percent or so who enter blindly. The money helps cover the cost of the office. Although the rent is low, I am a full-time volunteer, and my husband who maintains our website and heads our operations is also a volunteer, plus has a "real job." Any little bit helps to keep us moving along.

Do you accept online screeners?

We do accept them, but we do not recommend submitting an online screener. DVDs are more reliable and work for the majority of the group. But in fact we already have more online submissions this year, in the first two months of programming, than we did for the entire festival history. I think we are heading more and more towards an all-online submission world.

At the end of your selection process, do you only send a rejection notice or do you offer feedback?

I should and wish I could connect with every filmmaker! But right now, with the number of entries, and no volunteer to help with it, it isn't possible. If a filmmaker calls or emails, I will give whatever feedback is possible. I do contact all who are selected, invite them to the festival, and will give them as much information as I can.

Do you find media kits helpful when making decisions?

No, the programmers never see them.

What mistakes do filmmakers make when submitting to the Festival?

Not giving us clear ways to communicate with them. Some filmmakers fill out the form slap-dash and it is unreadable, so I never get a valid email address from them. I would also say I think they should look at the Festival's previous year's "Official Selections" before deciding to send in their film — especially if they are paying a submission fee. If you have a horror film or highly sexual film, look at the trailers from and see if the Festival had horror or sexual films in their previous years. If not, chances are that's not a good place to submit your film.

Do you pay screening fees?

Yes, we did last year, for some features. It is very dependent on our budget and negotiations with various distributors. Last year we ended up in the red, so we definitely won't be paying screening fees again. After thinking it over, in the long run we would really rather start raising funds to pay filmmakers cash prizes than pay distributors' screening fees.

Does PFF offer jury or audience prizes?

Yes, we present a variety of jury and audience awards, as well as one I choose as the festival director. There are no cash prizes for the winners, but every filmmaker who attends receives a gift basket (one per film) and the winners receive a very nice engraved glass award.

Do you offer travel funds or lodging for filmmakers?

We offer hotel rooms for all filmmakers for as long as they want to stay in Prescott during the Festival. We can only pay for flights for the opening night film and maybe a special guest. A small regional airline supports us by providing some flights for filmmakers flying in from Los Angeles or Denver.

What elements do you think make for a successful film?

I think number one is the story. No matter what, storytelling must come first. One thing that is often overlooked is audio. Many filmmakers think if they can hear it while editing, it is going to be okay. But once it gets on the big screen, if there is bad audio or a very loud mix, the audience will lose interest. We tell our programmers to listen to the audio mix very carefully.

What conventions instantly attract you to a film?

For a narrative, I like something that surprises me. That is the whole reason for independent films — not being a cookie cutter film, and offering something new and fresh. It's why I loved *Solitary.* The film keeps you guessing from start to finish — I just love that in a film.

I also like the passion of independent documentary filmmakers. They put their heart into it; they create a language that is their own, and they present it in a manner that they feel deeply about.

When watching a screener, what are some signals that a film will not be a good fit for PFF?

Bad language is bad writing. I know the studio people do it all the time, but to me, there are more words in this world. Random swear words aren't going to make it, and most of my programmers hate bad language. The programmers are a part of the community and Prescott is a small conservative community of mostly retired people. Not to say that all our films are family friendly – that's not correct. If a film has a plot and location that supports the use of lots of swear words, then it's okay. But random f-bombs are, in my opinion, low brow.

How important is premiere status when choosing films?

For us, it's not important. That said, we get some premieres for short films.

We had one filmmaker that couldn't attend, so he sent a friend in his place. The friend reported back that she was treated so well, that the filmmaker decided that we could have the world premier of his feature, which he is shooting right now.

Are you influenced by accolades or awards films win at other festivals?

Not really. Even though I get most of the selections from other events, I do not pay attention to what awards were garnered. Again, I am looking for films that fit our audience.

Are you influenced by famous names associated with a film?

I think at this point, if I see a film with a big name, they will probably ask for a screening fee — which we cannot pay. So I won't ask for it.

So in a sense, you are influenced, but not in a typical way. By not considering a film because of the possible screening fee, your decision to program was influenced.

I guess so. In the same vein, since I choose a lot of films from what others are programming, my decisions are influenced by them, also.

Do you choose films based on their own merit, or on how an audience will appreciate them?

I think on their merits. Last year, we screened a film full of curse words. I know I said that was a taboo for us, but it was just an amazing film. You didn't know what the ending would be until the end — and it just shocked you. The film, *KREWS*, ended up winning the jury award for Best Director. That said, I think the films I like are the films our audience would like. I chose to live in Prescott because I "fit in" so perhaps I *am* the audience. Also, I know that if we find a film about horses, it will draw a big crowd because Prescott is a historic Western town and folks here are horse crazy. So I guess I try to balance both the merits of the film and our audience.

How much do you think about your audiences when selecting films?

It is pretty important because if you have an empty theater, why bother doing a festival?

Do your donors or sponsors have any influence on programming decisions?

None.

How do you schedule your films, and does that schedule influence the films you ultimately program?

We start in the morning with family movies, then the afternoon with teen movies, and in the evening, more grown up films. Family films are often difficult to find.

Would you program a film that is not a perfect match for the family showcase just because you need to fill that slot?

Probably.

There's nothing wrong with that. I don't think many filmmakers understand the pressures and constraints festival programmers are under. If your schedule allows for five family films, then that is all you are able to program. There is no place for a sixth or seventh unless the whole schedule is reworked.

Yes.

How many other film festivals are in your area? Do you cooperate or compete with them?

There are Phoenix, Flagstaff, and Sedona. Tucson has a couple, and Scottsdale has one, plus the student film festivals. IFP Phoenix also has mini-festivals with their 48 Hour film challenges.

When I started, I was a little naïve. I thought all festivals just naturally worked together. Then I discovered there is a lot of competition for things like premiere status. I was, however, correct on Sedona: that they would do exactly what they ended up doing by mentoring and helping us out. Patrick Sweiss is amazing! But I didn't know that other festivals were not doing already that for one another.

I cooperate with everybody who asks; I've heard that other film festivals have not done that with each other, so I am hoping I am opening doors. There is one festival in my area that is extremely standoffish but now I have Phoenix and Sedona really cooperating with me, helping me out a lot and that is very valuable.

Do you try to show films no one else is showing?

I try not to show those that are already screening in Arizona unless they are off the charts. As I said, Prescott is a western town, so any movie that has anything to do with horses, the audience will stampede to see it. Phoenix showed a horse movie, then I showed it — and it was a really good seller.

Are you an Academy-considered festival? Do you think Academy accreditation is important to filmmakers or audience members?

We are not Academy accredited, but yes I do think it's important and I would love for it to have that happen. One of our board members would like to see that happen. She was one of the earliest founders of the Sundance Film Festival and has taken the task of growing us so we can obtain accreditation as her mission. We will see.

With all of the festivals out there, how is a filmmaker to know which ones are best to enter?

Word of mouth is the biggest thing, followed by what is important to you. Look online for festival chatter, and speak to other filmmakers who have played the circuit.

And every filmmaker and film festival director should be required to watch the movie *Official Rejection.* because it is a great study in what not to do. I literally watched the film ten times because it taught me so much. Then I went to Phoenix and saw the film again with three board members because the director, Paul Osborne, was going to be there. I spoke with him after the film and garnered even more information.
Yeah, we all want to get into Sundance as our first pick, but for the 99.99 percent of films that won't make that lofty goal, look at the smaller festivals that will give you the input you need, and the one-on-one treatment a big festival can't offer.

Why should filmmakers apply to the Prescott Film Festival, rather than others?

Because we have really great audiences. Filmmakers always tell us that the audience was fabulous, and the Festival treated them like gold — which is what they want. Prescott is a beautiful little mountain community and even if you don't win an award you get to stay in an amazing, fun, and friendly place. Our screening locations are great. We have a green room with snacks and coffee so filmmakers can network one on one.

Besides the screening, what do filmmakers get out of your film festival?

We try to give media exposure to as many of the films as possible. Many get reviews in the local papers, radio station exposure and a connection with a local television station, which broadcasts their interviews to cities outside of Prescott. At the green room, they can sit around on couches and be comfortable and talk with each other.

Networking is really important to us. There are after-parties every night at restaurants all over town where they can mingle. Last year, a talent agent came to the Festival and had a blast! The filmmakers he met now have a real connection a Hollywood talent agent — who is excited to work with them.

What should filmmakers bring to a film festival?

Respect and pride in the independent film art and industry. Whether documentary or narrative, help us get the word out about how amazing independent film is! In this community, we are still fighting the perception that indie films are shot in someone's back yard, and that all of the characters are mutilated in the end. Wear your festival badge proudly, and strike up conversations with locals about the art form!

What do you think filmmakers should do before arriving at a festival?

They should market their film to the press and our audience while here. We can only do so much to market each film.

Do you have a favorite success story?

Stephanie Argy (co-writer and co-director of *The Red Machine*) is the best marketer on the planet. We showed her film in 2009, and she and her crew handed postcards to every person they met, cold-called the TV station (and got an interview), and built a following on Facebook. Since then, they have kept at it, marketing away, taking the film to festivals all over the world, and building awareness through Facebook. It all paid off, and now they are booking the film in theaters across the country.

Failures. We all have them. What is one major blunder you've learned from?

Last year, due to a funding situation, we moved the Festival from the summer to the winter. Big mistake — Prescott is in the mountains and is a summer destination for residents of Phoenix and Tucson. In the winter, getting an audience together was not easy. So we moved it back to the summer. Losing a little bit of funding was not worth losing the larger amount of revenue we get through ticket sales.

What is one of the worst comments a filmmaker has ever said to you?

Oh, I remember this! A guy wanted to submit to the 2010 festival, but didn't get me the screener until after the Festival! I was going to put it in for consideration for the next year's festival, until he sent me a nasty email about how I treated filmmakers horribly, and to take his film out of consideration. It was very insulting, so I tried to send him an apology and explained what had happened, but he turned around and called me a liar. He is off the list.

Which brings me to my next question: Do you have a secret blacklist?

No. I haven't been around long enough to have a blacklist, I guess.

I have heard the horror stories about filmmakers or celebrities who come to town and bring along their children or entourage, and expect first-class airfare, meals, accommodations, etc. for everyone.

I can usually judge by emails and conversations if someone is going to be a problem. If anyone is difficult to work with, I will not extend an invitation to the Festival. I am a volunteer, and ultimately, I am here to make sure everyone has a good time, promote quality independent film, and not deal with nonsense.

What is the nicest compliment a filmmaker has ever told you?

One filmmaker left Prescott and called me to tell me his experience was very similar to the early days of Sundance. Years ago he had attended an after-party there and he sat next to Quentin Tarantino. After our festival he left wondering which new Quentin Tarantino he had interacted with at Prescott.

What have the advances in technology brought to the films you are now reviewing?

The image quality has improved considerably. Even when you compare the films between 2008 and 2009 to the ones we received in 2011, the picture quality is markedly improved.

Has the proliferation of film schools effected the quality of films submitted to PFF?

I think it has been positive. Sedona has a film school that is linked to Yavapai College's Zaki Gordon Film School. It is a good school, and there are students of all ages with a faculty that is honest enough to tell them, "hey, this is crap," or "this could be a masterpiece!" Sometimes they are right, and sometimes they are not, but all new filmmakers need some direction. For instance, I had an elderly man submit a film that he created on his own. It was from the heart, but horrible. The voiceover was a friend in the kitchen yelling over the action, "and then this happened." He needed direction, and I think a little schooling or a class would benefit him and others.

Has your job jaded your opinion of film or expanded your knowledge?

Expanded my knowledge. Definitely.

What three words best describe what you do?

1. Look at films
2. Worry about money
3. Interact with filmmakers

Finally, if you could give one piece of advice to someone who wanted to enter your film festival, would it be?

Write clearly on the form.

"DREAM BIG. NEVER SETTLE. GIVE EVERYTHING." ROBERTA MARIE MUNROE

Producer and Film Consultant
Former shorts programmer, Sundance Film Festival (2002-2006)
robertamunroe.com

Between 2001 and 2006, Roberta Munroe worked at Sundance as the Short Film Programmer. It was under her guidance that the organization flourished, receiving several reputable Webby Awards for their Online Film Festival.

Now working as a highly respected film consultant, Roberta lectures at notable universities including Columbia University, South Carolina Film Commission and Trident Tech College. Her book, *How to Not Make A Short Film: Secrets from a Sundance Programmer* has remained an Amazon best seller since its publication in 2009. Her one-on-one interactions with filmmakers and her passion for unique stories have made her a well-regarded and respected expert in her field.

From the moment we met, we realized we had met our match. Roberta and I have similar thoughts on filmmaking — from the importance of writing to the necessity of watching others' films. When I called to interview her, I knew she would end up steering the car — and she did. But what an amazing ride!

So, how do you want to proceed? In your role as a festival programmer, short film producer, or as a festival juror?

Let's start with producing and consulting. The first question a filmmaker asks me is, "How long should my short be?" The first question they should be asking is, "What makes a good short film story?"

Right now I have a director whose short I've produced — and it's 17 minutes long. When we got down to the final edit, I said, "We do not need this entire story line. This whole scene could get cut, and the film would be so much tighter, much more interesting, and easy to throw onto the festival circuit because it will be maybe, 12-13 minutes all in, including credits." He thought back before, when the original edit was 22 minutes, then as a team, we got it down to 17, and now I wanted to get it down to 13. He fought me on it, and ultimately launched picture with credits at 16:43. It got rejected from the top-tier festivals that I submitted it to, and it got rejected from festivals I really thought it would've played well at. And unfortunately, sometimes it can be all about the length of the film that makes or breaks your chances to be selected.

I talk about it in my book, *How Not To Make A Short Film*, and I talk about it ad nauseam in my talks, in my workshops, and in Master Classes — and at the end of the day if your short film is not economically crafted, you are dead in the water. For a feature, you have more leeway; you can meander a little bit more, audiences are used to sitting through ninety to 105 minutes for indie work. But when it comes to shorts, I think the marketplace is very different than it was even five years ago. The marketplace is saturated with high-quality, well-produced, sometimes well-written, sometimes well-acted shorts that are eight to twelve minutes.

When filmmakers ask me, "Roberta, as someone who's watched like 20,000 shorts, what is the right length for a short?" I always say your short should be as long as it takes to tell the story — without hyperbole, without pretty establishing shots, without crane shots, without overhead — without bullshit. And when I say bullshit, I don't mean that your shots of a gorgeous, lush valley on our way to our protagonist's house aren't beautiful. It is beautiful — it's just not pertinent to the story.

And it's a short. You don't need to establish that there's a beautiful valley surrounding the hundred miles around this person's house. You need to establish who this person is, and that can be done within the location itself. So you want to come up to the front door? Okay. You want to have the protagonist open the door for somebody? Okay. But that's going to take all of two seconds. Your opening sequence with this drive through the beautiful meadow, valley, or New York City, or the Rocky Mountains —whatever the fuck it is — who cares? At the end of the day that opening takes between 45-90 seconds, and I should know what this film is about within the first ninety seconds — two minutes tops.

If I don't know what's happening within the first two minutes of your film, you've lost me — and most programmers — and you only get one chance to nail it. Anyone who puts in an opening sequence rarely nails it.

So, that's the long answer. The short answer to how long should my film be: a short should be eight to twelve minutes. And if it's a one-note joke, drop it down to six Don't tell me the joke six times, tell me the joke once. I only need to laugh once, and you'll nail it, and I'll think you're a genius — and you'll play everywhere.

I agree. I think that a three to four minute one-joke film is an automatic "yes!" I can't program enough of them. Because I have to put something after the 20-minute drama, that...genocide or whatever. You need that little mind eraser.

Right, right. There are plenty of examples of longer shorts that have killed it at the festival circuit, and won grand jury prizes all over the place. And they're often either documentaries or dramas. Untold stories with a significant investigation of character that is compelling, and fresh.

When you watch a *Bugcrush* or you watch a *Pariah*, you are brought into a story very quickly in both of those films. And the tone is set, the "what's going to happen next" feeling that you want to feel when you're watching a movie is there, and you buy in. They're well-produced by very talented people, who have had top-notch crew and talent on board. And, it pays off.
They all pay off in the end. You're not just watching some beautiful short for 30 minutes. You're watching a story that pays off in the end. Now, what pays off is certainly subjective, but there are some elements that stand and deliver and are immutable. And what pays off is that the audience discovers something they had no idea was going to happen — something that touches you so deeply in your heart that you can't help but be moved.

So, when you're making your film, and whether it's a documentary or a narrative, or an animation, or experimental — there's got to be something that's universal and compelling. My 65-year-old, white, straight, living-in-Eastern-Canada mother is going to like *Bugcrush*.

To be very honest, I probably work with a hundred filmmakers a year, of which three are really talented and are really going to move forward — and have everything it takes to do that. So that's three percent.

And that says a lot, since you're very picky about who you take anyway. What types of filmmakers do you want to work with?

When I work with filmmakers, either as their producer, writer-director, or consulting-producer, or a consulting client who's just sending their work via my website, I always look for people who seem like they gave everything. Because filmmakers who give everything often surround themselves with other people who give everything — they're able to get a high-quality crew and talent, which lead them towards a greater high-quality film short.

Those films tend to do better on the festival circuit because the filmmaker's done their homework — they've done their research, they've watched shorts online, they've attended festivals wherever they could, and watched the shorts programming. These usually go on to play some of the top ten short film-specific festivals as well as top-tier festivals that program shorts, and they watch to see what's being made.

And I deeply believe that a filmmaker must give everything — they're definitely someone who doesn't settle, who's willing to crawl over broken glass to get the best possible film that they can get. These are the people I want to work with. Then, if I like your script and I think it's tight, I think it's interesting, I think it's fresh, then I'll proceed. We'll hire a great casting director, have amazing talent, and get rolling.

Sadly though, even when you have amazing talent and a rock solid crew, sometimes the movie doesn't turn out too well. Recently, I produced a film where the filmmaker fell apart on set and was essentially directed by the actors themselves, the DP, the first AD, and me. It was confusing and embarrassing, and ultimately a nightmare. At the end of the day did we get the film in a can? Yes. Does it look okay? Yes. Is the story told? Yes. Is it going to play on the festival circuit? Yes (but probably because of the cast). And I feel like that was a really huge letdown for me as a producer. Thinking that I had sort of checked all of the boxes, and realized, later, retrospectively, that this director wasn't actually willing to give everything, wasn't actually willing to crawl over broken glass to get this film done. He was terrified from the beginning and hid it. It didn't all come out until we got on set, and the proverbial shit hit the fan. And that's why I urge all filmmakers to give everything — no settling, no shooting just because you don't have anymore time to work on the script, and no buying into your own personal fears around success and/or failure.

I had a client two years ago who read my book and she emailed me this really great note about how she loved the book and how helpful it was on her recent set. Evidently, by day two of a three-day shoot, she saw that everything around her was falling apart, and she shut down production. She said to me, "I would not have had that courage had I not read your book. And while I'm going to throw away the money that I spent so far, I'm not going to settle."

Did she finally finish it?

She did, and I'm sure it's going to do a hundred times better than that first one — because she didn't settle.

That is amazing and, frankly as a filmmaker, inspirational. It's hard in the moment to make the right decisions with all of the mounting pressures around you — especially for young or first-time filmmakers.

Every year, another amazing producer, Maureen Ryan, invites me to do a Master Class at Columbia University for first-year producing MFA students. They have already gone through the first round, and are now at Columbia for whatever trillion dollars a year they have to pay to be there. At the first class, I say to them, "You know there are 75 of you here in this room. One of you might get into Sundance. Five of you will get into top-tier festivals, and maybe fifteen of you will have a solid experience on the festival circuit. What are the other sixty of you going to do?"

And I know that these filmmakers want pat answers to "What are the top ten things that my shorts can be about? What are the top ten festivals I should submit to?" And I respond by asking, "Why don't you focus on the craft? Why don't you focus on what is actually going to get an amazing producer on board? What is actually going to get you talent that is worth their salt to buy into your script, to want to be these characters? Why don't you focus on that and then worry about Top Ten lists and festivals?"

And of course, I usually follow up by asking, "How many of you have seen ten shorts this week?" And it's a zero — a big fat zero. "How many of you have seen ten shorts this month?" A few hands go up. "How many of you have seen ten shorts in the past six months?" More hands go up. "How many of you have seen ten shorts in the last year?" All the hands go up. Then I qualify it, "That doesn't include those at the school I'm teaching at, that doesn't include your peers." And most of the hands go back down.

That is upsetting.

You think?! And I think to myself, "Who does that? In what other industry does a professional do zero research and close to zero homework and expect to succeed?" Panhandlers can make maybe $100 a day, but even they have done some research and know which corner to sit on, what the sign should say, and how to approach people.

I'm with you 100%. In a conversation I had yesterday with a prominent festival director, I asked what was the worst mistake a filmmaker could make, and he replied, "not knowing your competition." Every film being produced is your competition — you compete for audiences, festival slots, media coverage — and of course money to make your next project. If you don't know what you are up against, you are driving blind. Do you think there's a breed of filmmakers who rush through the process so they can get their film on the festival circuit faster?

I am working with a director now who, by the tone in his emails and voicemails, is rather pissed at me. They missed the Sundance deadline, they missed the Tribeca deadline, and they missed one for a regional festival that they would have played. They wanted to send in a rough cut, and this is a short that requires extensive special effects, sound design, and music for the story to be realized. After repeated pleas for me to help them make these deadlines, I told them I could walk the rough cut over to the programmer's house right now, but I didn't want to because it's not ready. Who gives a shit about this festival? There are a thousand festivals and maybe a hundred that matter — and they take place all year long. So what's the rush?

Yes, there are the big guys, and we all want to play the freezing cold, super sexy, alcohol-saturated Sundance in January, or the very well programmed European, Clermont-Ferrand in February, or the very chilly, but with excellent beer, Berlinale in February. But there others of equal value all year 'round. There are plenty more top tier festivals that you could show in. There's Oberhausen, there's DC Shorts, there's Palm Springs, there's Toronto Worldwide, there's HollyShorts — there's just so many places that your film can play every month. Again, why rush?

I know you were at Sundance for a while, and to many Filmmakers, that is the holy grail. What is the allure?

This year, 2012, at Sundance 7,765 short films were submitted, of which 64 were selected. Which, by the way, is twenty shorts fewer than they have shown annually in the last decade. So you have less than a .5 percent chance of getting into that festival. Why are you killing yourself to win the lottery? Because that's essentially what Sundance has become: a lottery. I'm sure that every year, at least 150 solid works of art did not show there because there's no room. Perhaps that's the allure? Being one out of almost 8,000?

So, if that's the case, what do you think's the real purpose of festivals?

There are a number of things, but, as clichéd as this might sound, the main purpose — whether you are an established award-winning director or a first-timer, is to meet other filmmakers, including producers, writers, and talent. It's the one place where everyone is together.

That is followed closely by seeing what quality of work is out there, and what other people are creating in terms of the art form. While it's important to understand the industry of filmmaking, it is also critical to understand the art and craft of filmmaking. Go to as many screenings as you can bear. Attend panels to find out what the up-and-coming trends are. And discover how others are doing with pre-sales and distribution.

By doing this, you create your community of filmmakers — like-minded people, who are going to be there for you. To read your scripts, to kick start a campaign, to provide you with a shoulder to cry on when you get rejected from a festival, or your wife leaves you or your dog dies — someone you met at a festival (writer's lab, etc.) knows what you're going through and can offer support.

I have always argued that filmmaking is not an individual art, but a community endeavor. A painter or sculptor can create alone in a studio. A filmmaker, with very few exceptions, must rely on the talents of others to see their vision through.

Bueno, only crazy people make movies. So it's critical to surround yourself with other like-minded crazy people. I mean, it's not very profitable, it's a lot of fucking work, it takes a year to realize any rewards from said work, except for the day-to-day rewards of just being an artist. And in the end, you are stuck with this product that you can no longer change.

Let's say I sold things — take this chair I am sitting in — the chair can be recovered every six months; it can come in red leather, wheels can be added, the style of the arms can be rounded. I can continue to modify it indefinitely, making upgrade after upgrade. But a film has about 12-18 months of shelf life before you have to make another one. Before you have to pick yourself up off the floor, of whatever floor you are lying on after you got rejected, or you got in and nothing happened, and you didn't get a manager, you didn't get an agent, all the things that you dreamed of didn't happen after you got into Sundance. There you are, back again, having to raise another $10-, $15-, $25,000 to make another short, or go the distance and raise however much you need for your low-budget feature. Or you'll go work on someone else's film, or you'll go work at the local indie bookstore.

And I would say ninety out of a hundred short filmmakers get a job, and the other ten move on and make another movie. Because you learn fairly quickly, that not only are you working with crazy people — myself included, yourself included — the pressure of creating art in the film industry is very different.

You're not by yourself with a canvas and paints, and deciding and changing and shifting and growing and emoting as an artist. The only time that you get to do that, really self-reflective, internal work is when you're writing the script. And once you've finished the script, or so you think, then you're out there in the world and you walk into any film set, there are another thirty people who are going to help you make this movie.

And that's when things start to get out of your hands, right? You have the vision, and you have to be willing to move, and shift, and grow, with that vision in mind at all times. With a DP who's drunk, with a producer who's breaking up with her girlfriend, with talent who hasn't eaten since yesterday. It takes everything! I've done it so many times, and by the end I think to myself, "It's a good thing that I'm insane! It's a good thing that I love this! It's a good thing that I'm an artist because who can do it?" But most importantly, I am grateful to be surrounded by other insane peeps — my community — who think directors sobbing their eyes out in the back seat of a picture car is just another day in the office.

Ha ha! I was wondering where you we going with that. And I couldn't agree with you more. Do you mind talking about the process at Sundance? I am asked all the time, "Are they really watching 7,200 films?"

Yeah.

In their entirety?

I will say I have no idea what other programmers are doing in the privacy of their own screening rooms. Having said that, I'm not going to lie to you, if your movie is not going to make it to the next round, that's going to be evident rather early on and if I had to watch every 47-minute "pride" documentary I'd be drinking more than I do now.

But seriously, the process at Sundance is just like the process at almost every other film festival: Watch the movie, write coverage (what's it about, how good/fresh was the story, casting, edit, etc.), share it with your colleagues, and grade the top ones and (often) collectively make decisions on who gets in and who gets a pass. When Mike Plante and I worked together, the ratings were one to four. So the ones and twos were passes, and the threes and fours were the ones we short listed — but we did indeed watch everything.

One time during the Festival, I was at the bar (where I usually am) talking to a filmmaker about how hard programmers will fight for a certain film — the entry made it through round one of the short list, round two of the short list, round five of the short list. The film kept staying in that top section of shorts that we really wanted to show that year. So the filmmaker asked, "So what you're telling me is, to get into a festival with such a high volume of submissions you have to have a champion on the programming team? Someone who just loves your film so much they're just not going to let it go?" Yes, that might be true. But what is most true is your film has to stand out from the crowd because there isn't a programmer alive who wouldn't agree that they've shown work they didn't like one bit, but it was so well crafted they were compelled to select it.

That's interesting. I find that the top-rated films from my first-round screeners usually do not appeal to me, and the ones that fall into the lower range of top-ranked films, completely speak to me and our audience.

I just watched a compilation of about 45 shorts from a top-tier festival last year, and there were about four good ones. And I thought, some of this stuff was so 1999 I couldn't believe it! I think that is partially due to the age of the programming staff. Younger programmers weren't around in 1999, so they don't know that this film has been made a hundred times. For them, it's fresh. I don't want to sound ageist, but I wonder if all programmers are doing their homework. Have they watched films and trends over the last ten years? Do they know what is truly fresh? Can they recognize new and forward-thinking talent?

I always profess that you don't have to spend $40,000 to make a short. You don't have to have Samuel Jackson in your short. But, what you want to do is reveal yourself as an artist — because that is something that is tangible, that is something I can see, or read, and feel. Programmers are human beings — we're not just programming with our brains — we're programming with our souls. So, again, when people ask, "What movie should I make?" Make the movie that you're passionate about that hasn't already been made a hundred times! With passion and research, your talent will show through, and you will see the rewards.

I sometimes feel, as programmers, sometimes we're a little too tough on some films. Or, we like films that, for whatever reason, no one else likes. I know that last year, the two of us loved Pioneer *by David Lowery.*

Pioneer is one of the top five shorts of the past decade.

I agree with you! We awarded it a jury prize at Ashland. But when I brought it to DC Shorts, the reaction from my audience was less fervent than I expected. I was expecting it to win the audience award, but the audience was not as impressed as they were with other films. Do you think we watch film with a different eye?

A great short I loved is *The River* by David Browles. The film had been rejected almost everywhere. I championed it to all the top-tier feature and short film festivals, because I loved that film. It has elements that feel almost like a play — the interior locations are sort of claustrophobic, which I really liked. Evidently, few others did.

So like all programmers, you have selected films you loved, but the audience didn't see what you saw.

Oh my God — every single year, every year. Mike and I would know which ones, too. We'd think, this is a really good film and people are going to hate it. I think it's important to expose an audience to films they wouldn't necessarily see any other way.

I think most programmers would agree. If I have a thousand selections and they all are mediocre, then I have to pick the best of the mediocrity for my audience. As a festival director, I'm constantly trying to market my festival to filmmakers. I see too many festivals aren't necessarily doing so, instead they're hoping that their buzz will carry them.

Well, here's the harsh reality: at the end of the day, there are, at maximum, two hundred stellar short films on the circuit. Programmed together, it could make a really solid festival. The larger short film festivals show about three hundred. How many do you show?

We show about 140-150.

So you're picking the cream of the crop, hopefully. Then the question is, how do you get to be one of those 150 filmmakers? What have you done? What have we talked about earlier?

What do you think about storytelling vs. schooling? I met a filmmaker the other day, son of a friend of mine, who is making these personal docs about things he's doing in his life. They're amazing! He's a photographer, they look good. But he was really able to, without studying story structure, create compelling stories that made me want to see more.

And he'll probably go the distance because I bet he is consumed with the work. Like I said, you have to be prepared to walk through broken glass.

Though one alarming trend I see at schools is the sense of entitlement some are teaching to students. I was on a panel and a filmmaker stood up and said, "Is it true that Sundance has a bias against this particular film school?" I responded, "I don't think so. I think that all film festivals have a bias against bad filmmaking." So, if a film is good, regardless of what school you come from, you have a chance.

What are some of your favorite experiences at other festivals?

In 2010, I was asked to give a Master Class at the Saint John's Women's Film Festival, at the eastern-most tip of North America. Also programmed was a Master Class with Christine Vachon [author of *A Killer Life: How an Independent Film Producer Survives Deals and Disasters in Hollywood and Beyond.*] So, this special group of filmmakers, most of whom were local, had the opportunity to interact on a very individual level with Christine! As an up-and-coming producer, I was as excited as they were — it was one of the best five days that I've spent at a festival. The organizing group of the Festival were amazing because they gave everything. The filmmakers had an amazing time because they were treated so well. We were fawned over by the local press, which no matter how local and how small it is, it feels good that someone gives a shit about your art, right?

That is incredible. And that's why I still go to festivals whenever I can — the connections. You mentioned press. I know that as a festival director, I am always looking for opportunities to connect the media and filmmakers, but often, it ends up with less-than-stellar results.

I've been with filmmakers at top-tier festivals, where I'm either representing or have produced their film, and the publicist comes forward with a list of people who are interested in interviewing them, and they don't want to talk to, or they don't feel like it's important to talk to *The Salt Lake Tribune*, or some small community newspaper — or some blogger whose reach is only 150 people. And I always counter with, "Are you out of your fucking mind? You have the opportunity to hone the craft of talking about your film, to understand what it is that people find interesting about your movie. To have the opportunity that maybe, some Roberta Munroe, or Christine Vachon, just happens to come across that blogger's blog, or they're my best friend, or they're the boyfriend to the assistant of some big William Morris agent, and they send this blog link all over the place." I don't care about your ego. Give everything, everywhere,

Especially now that the media's all online anyway, a Google hit is still a Google hit. They all add up, which helps you spread your message. You'd be crazy not to do it. Like you said, it's practice. Yes, you might practice on The Salt Lake Tribune *for your* New York Times *interview.*

I get very, very bored and I have a very short fuse with the uninspired, ego-driven filmmakers who think they can't waste their time on the small stuff. The grateful shall inherit the world.

What's the biggest mistake you think filmmakers make when they're submitting to a festival?

I would say the top three are: 1) they're submitting to the wrong festival — a festival that doesn't show their genre of work, 2) they spend too much money on these festival submissions, and over-submit, and 3) the film is not ready for submission. They rushed to send in a mix hoping programmers will forgive the missing effects, or the missing sound mix, or the missing whatever. If it is integral to the film, they will not. I think the lack of a strategy for festivals is a major issue that few discuss openly.

When I meet filmmakers with new films, they usually tell me that they are going to send it to Sundance and Tribeca and Toronto. I retort that, since they have a snowball's chance in hell of getting in, instead of sending to 15 festivals with no chance of getting into, research and find the five you know you can *get into. Save the money and heartache of rejection letters, and instead, start getting acceptance letters.*

The other events might not be huge festivals, but they're the ones where you're actually going to meet audiences, and have the ability to talk to film people and interact. That's why I love small regional festivals, I think so much more gets done at those than the big guys.

Okay, conversely, what's the one thing a filmmaker can do for their best chances?

Other than having a great movie? I would say the number one thing is to do your research, talk to filmmakers who have already been at the festival you're submitting to. Doing so will save you money, time and effort. And better zero you in on the festivals where you really have a chance. Because playing at (the very fictitious!) Roberta Munroe's Monthly Film Screening Series in Torrance,

California may garner you more positive energy for your film than screening at a top-tier festival where all the people you want to meet are focused on feature films.

Daniel Sol from HollyShorts emailed and asked for me to send a few films I was working on for his monthly showcase. It's an opportunity for films to be seen by an audience, receive feedback, and take the temperature of the room. Even though you might have locked picture, you can and should go back to reshape if you can, right?

So I approached two filmmakers. One was stoked and said, "Sweet! Thank you so much!" The other filmmaker was like, "No thanks. I'm going to wait until their actual festival." The former went to the screening, and it was great. He got feedback, saw that the audience was really into his film, and they had ideas about what made the film work, and where it didn't. The latter's myopic approach cost her the chance she ultimately wanted.

Why would you say no to a monthly screening series? You're going to have thirty to sixty people in the audience and get feedback on your film. It seems like a no-brainer. Particularly since she was in the fine-tuning process of locking the picture anyway."

Yeah, that's crazy. Again it goes back to community. The audience is part of that community. You are making art for them to enjoy, so why not get them involved in the process? I could talk to you all day. Which is why I love bumping into you on the circuit. So if you could describe what you do in three words, what would they be?

How about six words? Dream big. Never settle. Give everything.

"YOUR FILM IS NOT FOR EVERY FESTIVAL." JON GANN

Founder and Former Festival Director, DC Shorts Film Festival
Owner, ReelPlan, filmmaker and festival consulting

About the Festival:

- Founded in 2004, the DC Shorts Film Festival turns the spotlight on truly independent short films, created by new and established filmmakers in an era when the art of filmmaking is opening to all.
- 11-day regional event for general audiences
- Website: dcshorts.com

The last chapter turns the interview towards me. While I was planning the interviews, a friend recommended that I interview myself. Knowing that attempt would only end in a mess, I called upon my friend, Kelley Baker.

Kelley Baker is an independent filmmaker based in Portland, Oregon, and the writer and director of three indie feature films: *Birddog*, *The Gas Cafe*, and *Kicking Bird*. He specializes in creating extreme low-budget narrative films (i.e.: guerilla filmmaking), usually bending a few rules to get the job done.

Kelley has spent the past few years touring the U.S. teaching his unique and scrupulous brand of filmmaking at workshops and showing his films to audiences at art house theaters, colleges, universities and media art centers. While on his last tour, he took the time to call, start the recorder, and turn the interview on me...

KELLEY: I know that you're the founder of DC Shorts. How long has DC Shorts been around and why did you create the Festival?

JON: The long story is that I was — I am a filmmaker. I guess I don't make films anymore, but I'm still a filmmaker. Like you're always a doctor. Anyway, in 2001, I had a film that literally played around the world — about fifty festivals. At the time, it was the most successful gay-themed, short film ever. So I took the year off and traveled around the planet to attend festivals. Maybe because it was a short, I was treated poorly at many festivals, and I realized that a lot of the bigger festivals seemed to be about money and sponsors and parties — and filmmakers, unless you were Woody Allen, were not really important. And if you made short films, it seemed like you were completely ignored. All I wanted was to find a community of filmmakers and to reach audiences. I wanted to meet the people who watched my film to find out what they liked and didn't like, so I could learn before I made another one. But the more I traveled, the more I found it increasingly difficult to get what I wanted.

Towards the end of my run, I went to Ashland, Oregon for the Ashland Independent Film Festival. It was their first year — and it happened to be two weeks after 9/11. I took one of the first flights I could get out of Washington, D.C. and made my way across the country.

Maybe it was because of the post-9/11 love-fest feeling, or maybe it was because they didn't exactly know what they were doing because it was an inaugural event — but it was the most amazing festival I had ever had been to. Everything was structured to be about community: bringing the community together to watch films; filmmakers meeting one another and seeing each other's work; filmmakers sharing and exchanging ideas. I met filmmakers and organizers that weekend that I still talk to on a regular basis — and I try to attend Ashland every year. It is amazing to see how it has grown into one of the most important regional festivals in the country.

When I came back to D.C., through a series of very fortunate events, I had access to a new black box theater space. I was beginning my quest to "out" the local film community. Washington, D.C. is home to one of the largest film and video industries in the country, but because of the nature of the work — news, government films, and political spots — few people talked about their work. I realized that in order to build a community of filmmakers I wanted to interact with, I needed to attract them. And what better way than through a festival to show their independent works?

I called a good friend of mine, Gene, who is the Ethel to my Lucy, and pronounced, "We're going to put together a film festival!" We put a call for entries out to local filmmakers, as well as the dozens that I met during my festival circuit. We ended up with 78 entries, which I thought was an amazing start. As the event grew nearer, I became ever more nervous, as I realized I was paying for this shindig out of my checkbook, and what would happen if no one showed up? I had to sell 200 tickets to break even, but the theater only seated eighty people, and we only had three shows — which meant I had to sell out nearly every seat! I was freaking out (as I still do before every event) but discovered that I did not have to — at the first show, there was a line out the door and around the corner. We added more chairs, breaking every fire code in D.C., and crammed people into the small space. When the lights came on, the applause from the audience — and more importantly, the reaction from the 33 filmmakers in attendance — proved that the event was a huge success.

It's been a runaway success every year since. Last year, we showed 145 films from 23 countries. We're now the third largest shorts event in the country — the biggest outside of California.

Can you tell me about your selection process? How does it work? How did you develop it?

I am very proud to have built a unique process — an open process — in which every entrant has the ability to see the judges' raw scores and comments. As a filmmaker, I was bewildered by the decisions made by some programmers, and frustrated that many would not explain their decisions or give any insight into their process.

About six months from the deadline, we open our submission period. Like most festivals, we use Withoutabox because the call for entries reaches a large number of filmmakers, and the data collection is already done for us. However, I feel that their application process is a little intensive for first-time filmmakers and people who just want to submit a short piece they did on the fly.

Anyway, after receiving the DVD or online screener URL in the office, we enter the filmmaker's information into a proprietary system we built to score, comment and select films. All films are removed from their packaging and placed in uniform sleeves with a barcode identifier so we can track it through the process.

We assign about two-hours of film to teams of volunteer first-round screeners, who we train on our aesthetic, review writing, the scoring system, and about themes we are actively looking to program. Last year, we had about 130 screeners.

Our screeners are people who have attended the Festival in the past, who have volunteered for the Festival in the past, general audience members, filmmakers, industry people — from all walks of life — and for the most part, they are people who love film, and love DC Shorts. I feel that if someone loves film and would shell out $15 to see your short in a theater, they are perfectly capable of expressing an opinion.

We strip all films of all identifying marks, take them out of all packaging, put them in generic sleeves, and assign a barcode. They are randomly assigned to teams of three, where they are watched in their entirety. We have an online judging system which we have built, where judges can score films, recommend some for a second committee, or second opinion, and they may leave a comment.

Towards the end of that process, a second team watches the top scorers, as well as those that might have been recommended, and a few others I might have personally invited along my travels on the festival circuit.

I spend about three weeks watching 300+ films and deciding the line-up of 120 to 150 films. At the end of our process — this is the thing I'm most proud — we open up the system to all the filmmakers. Along with your acceptance or rejection letter, you also have access to our website to see the judges' scores and comments. I think that's really useful information. I believe that if you're paying to enter a film festival, you should have some sort of feedback, and you should at least find out what the screeners were thinking.

I know many festivals, especially the ones I've been talking to for this book, have the time and consideration to do this — but most don't. The only reason we can do it is because we have this amazing system we built that, hopefully, we will soon be licensing to other film festivals. I hope that it will become the standard, rather than the exception.

Well, you said something that I find fascinating. You said that the first round they watch the entire film. Don't most film festivals do that?

Before I started this book I thought that, too. I'm finding more and more festivals are actually watching films in their entirety. Some might know after twenty minutes of a feature or ten minutes of a short that it's nothing they're ever going to program.

It's interesting, some festivals receive thousands of films. Watching that many submissions can be daunting, and it may be hard to believe that they are being watched without rushing or prejudice. But I have to take the word of my fellow programmers when they say they watch the films. I trust them, I know their personalities and I know their dedication to film.

How much time does that take to watch the films?

Well, I'm only really watching the top three hundred or so, and I also watch the bottom fifty, because the bottom fifty are the ones that call and complain the most. It's like a three or four week period, five or six hours at a time.

That's a commitment.

It is a commitment, but I am only watching submissions for a few weeks. I know of programmers that all they do — all day long — is watch films. They get in at 9:00 am, they do an hour's worth of emailing and catching up, and then they sit down and watch six to eight hours of film almost every day.

Let me ask you, changing gears a little bit. As a filmmaker, what do I get if your festival decides to screen my film?

Hopefully, we can give you the connection with an audience you don't get anywhere else. I know everyone does Q&A's at the screenings, and we do too. I think our audiences are very smart and really appreciate the form. We host lots of parties that all have special quiet areas for filmmakers where they can actually talk to people. It's fun to party your ass off, but I also think it's important to have time to talk and connect.

If you can get to Washington, we'll house you, we'll feed you, we make sure you have access to every screening you want to attend, and every party you want to attend. We make sure you have all of the other filmmakers' contact information so you can keep in contact with them in the future.

So, do you think that, are you the exception here, or is this the norm? I know that back in the day, many years back, film festivals would pay to bring filmmakers out. Is that not happening anymore?

Some of the bigger festivals have travel budgets. I wish we did, but we cannot raise the kinds of funds necessary to do so. Even without travel funds, last year, we had 130 filmmakers attend. Fortunately we are timed towards the end of the Toronto International Film Festival, so there are a few filmmakers who will come to D.C. because they're already on the East Coast.

Also, I think our prominence has made it necessary for some filmmakers to attend. We have become an important festival on the circuit, therefore they have to show. When I was traveling to forty film festivals a year, maybe three of them paid for me to attend. I had to pay the rest of my way. Most of them gave me rooms and food, but I was booking the flights to Italy, and France, and Tokyo myself. To me, that was an expense in making my film — just as important as my catering or tape stock budget. If festivals were to be my distribution method, I had to make the investment to meet with the other filmmakers and build a community. So when I raised money to make the film, I raised a load of money for me to travel.

Well then let me ask you this because I know this is something you're very sensitive to. I just spent all this money making my film. Why do I have to pay an entry fee? If I call you, will you waive the entry fee?

Film festivals are not cheap to run. And because most of them are once-a-year events, all the income is generated in a short, maybe two-week period. That means zero cash flow for fifty weeks of the year. For most festivals, entry fees are a way to bring a tiny amount of money in throughout the year. The truth is most entry fees, by the time you've paid Withoutabox, between the marketing fees and commissions, you are remitted a very small amount back.

I think for some festivals — and for me too — it's a gate keeping device. If filmmakers have to start thinking about which festivals to enter and decide where to spend their money wisely, they might actually start picking the festivals that are more appropriate for their film. Filmmakers who blank submissions — send films to the big names or ones they think they have to pay — often end up submitting films which are not relevant to the festival's mission or previous programming decisions.

Filmmakers have to really figure out where their film is appropriate, and target those specific festivals as opposed to just thinking, "I'm going to win Sundance with this." Well, chances are you're not — they received 8,200 submissions last year for about sixty slots. So, it's probably not going to happen.

You're telling me that I have to research film festivals, but how do I tell what's a credible film festival and what isn't? How do I know I'm not getting ripped off?

Online research will only get you so far. It's easy to come up with a slick website. I've seen some sham film festivals with really slick websites, just as I've seen some legitimate festivals with horrific websites. It's really about communicating with other filmmakers. Use Facebook, Twitter, message boards, and listservs — they're great resources to communicate with other filmmakers who have attended festivals and find out, "What did you think of this one? Was it worth the time and effort? Did you really like it or not?" I mean, festivals are always going to toot their horn and say how great they are, but if you were actually to talk to other filmmakers — they are your greatest resource.

And for God's sake — get out to other film festivals! Talk to filmmakers with films that are similar to yours and ask, "Well, where else did you apply? Where did you play? Where did you get rejected from?" If they loved a film festival, they're going to tell you. Just as they're going to tell you how much they disliked a festival that didn't treat them right.

When I ask my students to research festivals, I always come back and ask, "What kind of films are they looking for?" Sometimes it's obvious: DC Shorts takes any film under 20 minutes. But other film festivals are less specific.

Look for festivals that put their catalogs or list of past films online. If you can't find a catalog, e-mail the festival office and request one so you can see what they've screened in the past. Most festivals will be happy to share catalogs with you because that's the single most reliable source of information.

DC Shorts just launched an area on our website where anyone can watch 200 films that we've shown in the past. Now, submitters can see some of the films we've shown in the past, and hopefully realize, "Oooh, this is the type of comedy they like," or "Wow, they don't seem to program horror, so maybe my slasher film is not for their audience."

I know when filmmakers are done with post-production, they're tired. They're kind of "over it," and just want success to happen. But, just like you had a plan on the pre-production side, you have to plan your distribution — especially if you want the festival circuit to be that distribution. There are very few films that are so great that festival directors traveling from festival to festival say, "Oh my god, I have to have that film!" It happens to a few, but for the most part, filmmakers really have to put in the work,

Do you invite films, then, to your festival?

I do. I don't invite a lot, but I do invite a few. Throughout the year, I might see a film here and there that I will reach out to and invite them to apply. But those films have to go through the same process as everyone else. I learned a long time ago that if I programmed a film that I loved without going through the process, the audience ultimately won't like it.

Wow. That's an interesting thought.

I talked to Roberta Marie Munroe about this. I think that programmers look at films in a completely different way than the audience does. I look for unique story elements or a creative way to approach a story, while I think my audience just wants to be entertained for ninety minutes.

Last year I programmed a film, *Pioneer* by David Lowery, that Roberta and I awarded a jury prize at another festival. We both agree that it is probably one of the best short films we've seen in the past few years. The audience reaction was so-so. They seemed to enjoy it, but not enough to win an audience award or mention. And when I spoke to attendees, they thought I was crazy for loving it so much. Go figure.

What's the biggest mistake that a filmmaker can make when submitting a film to your festival?

When I sit on panels or speak to filmmakers, I always start by listing five things to do to guarantee *not* getting into a festival:

1. *Don't read the submission rules or guidelines*
2. *Ignore all deadlines*
3. *Beg for a fee waiver*
4. *Don't bother protecting your disc for shipping*
5. *Send us a film completely inappropriate for our audience*

Do the opposite and you have the key to success. Seriously — it really is that simple. And it all comes back to doing the research.

There are rules for a reason. A lot of them are boilerplate, but some of them are very specific, like "don't send us a media kit." Media kits are automatically thrown in the trash without looking at them — we don't have the space to store them, we don't have time to read them. I'm not particularly interested in what you have to tell me, because whether you won Sundance or have never played another festival before makes no difference to my first round screeners who will never see these expensive materials. They watch and review your film on its own merits.

Don't send DVDs in paper sleeves in a non-padded envelope — it's going to show up in a dozen pieces. In our rules, we tell you how to properly pack your entry. I know it sounds ridiculous, but it guarantees the disc gets here unscratched and unharmed.

The rules have the dates for all of the deadlines and announcements. I can't answer twenty emails a day asking, "When are you making announcements?" It's on the website in bold and large type if you were to read it.

These are mistakes that I want to avoid while submitting, but what are the mistakes filmmakers make when they attend a film festival?

You can't be a wallflower. You have to go out there and work it. Reasons to attend a festival include 1) finding out what the audience thinks of your film, 2) making connections to help with making your next film or films, and 3) seeing your competition.

Gauge how an audience reacts to your film. I'm really impressed and amazed when I watch an audience watching my films, because, inevitably, they laugh at the things I don't think are funny. I need to understand what that's about. Which is why, when my film is on the screen, I turn around and watch the audience. I don't need to watch the film — I've seen it before. But I have never seen this audience's reaction.

And you have to work an audience, too. You have to have postcards and gimmicky things, to build an audience. Festivals do their best to try and attract a wide audience, but honestly, with dozens or hundreds of films, we can only promote a handful to the press. If your film is very specific to an audience, try and do some research before you attend a festival and market while you're there. If your film is about fetishists, see if that city has a fetish bar, and go and hand out your postcards there.

The second main reason you go to festivals is to meet filmmakers. Meet, exchange, laugh — and build friendships that will last a long time. That's really important. There are filmmakers I have met over the years at other festivals who I speak with all the time. They have become my touchstone for new projects — and I always have incredible sources to find other filmmakers through their friends.

And, third, you have to see your competition. You have to see what other films are out there. What are other filmmakers making? How are they making them? What new techniques are they using? Because, ultimately, you are competing against hundreds, if not thousands, of other films for slots at festivals. You've got to know what your competition is doing. Do you think professional athletes stay home and have no idea what the opposing teams' stats are? No — they watch tapes, study the competition, and create an appropriate game plan.

You just said something about, "You need to come to a festival to promote the film." I thought film festivals are supposed to promote my films.

For DC Shorts, our biggest expense after rent is public relations. We spend a lot of money on PR. But because we do, we're mentioned in every major paper, TV station, blog, local magazine and other media. The strategy pays for itself — we have sold out theaters. But one of the reasons we fill theaters is because filmmakers are out there hitting the pavement too. The majority of our audience comes to more than one screening, because even though they only intended to come to one screening, they're having such a good time and they're meeting filmmakers who say, "You've got to come see this film that I made," that they come back for more. Every bit helps.

Now, I'm not saying promotion is completely the responsibility of a filmmaker. I've heard of some horrible sham festivals in which that was the expectation — where the festival did no promotion of their own, and said to the filmmakers, "Well, you're here, so you take care of this." That is an unfair expectation to ask of a filmmaker.

How do I engage with an audience so that I make sure that I'm doing stuff that's okay? That's not going to piss you off?

For the most part, whatever you're going to do short of lighting yourself on fire, I'm sure is going to be fine. As long as you're not defacing property, not upstaging others, or causing traffic issues, I don't really have a problem. We've had some people do some crazy stuff in the past. I come from a marketing background, so to me, the more creative, the more I'm impressed.

Honestly, what pisses you off?

Not a lot (especially if the five rules were followed), but the biggest one is — while you are here, don't be a prima donna. I don't have time to baby sit you. I've prepared an entire week of activities, screenings, parties and panels for you to attend to meet other like-minded people. They're designed for all to enjoy equally.

And please don't come to me with crazy requests for special seats or a private tech rehearsal or an upgraded hotel room. All the seats in the theater are the same; the projection is fine because we've tested it multiple times; and unless there's an Oscar on your mantle, I can't scrape the funds together to pay for your mini bar habit. I have 140 other filmmakers to host at the same time as you — most of whom are patient and grateful for the opportunity to show their film to sold-out audiences.

Do you have a blacklist?

A formal one? No. Do I remember who was a pain in the ass? You bet. It is something I need to consider if I want the filmmaker to attend. If their film is incredible, I will just have to suck it up and be a gracious host. If the film is borderline, I would probably pass.

Do film festival directors talk to each other?

We do. A few years ago, I started a private Facebook group that has over 550 members. We communicate with one another, exchange ideas, and ask each other questions. Some of us attend each others' events, so we definitely connect there. The International Film Festival Summit hosts about 200 directors from really big events to small start-ups.

I don't think we necessarily influence each other, but I think we're always interested to see what each other programmed, and why we programmed it. I don't think that I would necessarily take a film just because it played a festival I respect, but I might give it a second look.

What types of films are you hesitant to program?

Our audience is not enamored with horror films. Suspenseful-scary will sometimes work. Non-gratuitous gore sometimes makes the cut. Humorous horror plays well. But torture porn or slasher films are not to their taste. The few times I tried to stick such a film in, I inevitably heard about it after the screening, and then spent a lot of time working to win back the audience.

What is your take on premiere status?

I'll be honest, for short films, I could care less about premiere status. A lot of festivals are changing their attitude about premiere status because there are so many festivals out there. If you're waiting on a place for your world premiere, you're probably going to be waiting for quite a while — especially if you're waiting for a big festival to take the world premiere.

I think most festivals are looking for state, or regional, or city premieres. I'd rather be the first festival in D.C. to show your film, but the truth is, I don't mind showing your film if it's been shown elsewhere in D.C. because that event has already done the work to get the press coverage — I can ride on their coattails.

And honestly, I don't think audiences really care one way or the other.

Now, features are a different beast. I think for some features, a premiere at a big festival means a lot, and some festival programmers are looking to score premieres because it's an interesting press connection for them.

In the book Selling Your Film Without Selling Your Soul, *I read that some filmmakers are getting paid to show their films at festivals. Is that common?*

It is more uncommon than common. Screening fees really vary depending on the festival. From what I've been discovering, screening fees are rare for domestic films, and they're more prevalent for foreign films, or films that come with a distributor attached. That's part of the distribution deal. I've only heard of one festival, in the whole world, that pays to show your short, and even then, you're talking a few dollars. Most festivals just don't have that kind of money.

On the niche festival circuit (LGBT, Jewish, Asian), there has been the practice of paying screening fees, but mostly for distributor-held, or foreign films.

Some studios want festivals to pay, especially for films with a big name. Many of the programmers I know will either pass on a film, or negotiate for a deal they can work with. Again, money is scarce, and while I understand that fees are important, they cannot always be paid as demanded.

You just mentioned big names in films. How hard is it going to get into festivals without a name?

Well, big names might get your DVD to the front of the line, but honestly I, and most people I know, will not program a film with a big name just because of the name. The film has to be of equal quality to everything else

I am programming. Now, I might take a film with a bigger name on it over another film if it's of exactly the same quality, and maybe the same story line. But, I'm not going to take a film with a star if the film just sucks. What's the point? I'll get the audience in, and they'll be so excited to see this film with star "X" in it, but then they'll watch it and say, "Well that film just sucked." I gained nothing, I probably pissed off my audience more than I entertained them.

If you're a filmmaker, having a name helps. If your strategy is to play the festival circuit, having a name doesn't really matter. If your strategy is to sell your film to a distributor, then a name really does help. But, if you know your film is only really going to go as far as the festivals — which is a hard pill to swallow because everyone is dreaming that their film is going to be picked up by a distributor and shown to multiplexes around the country, which doesn't happen that often — then don't worry about the name. Worry about the important stuff: friggin' good storytelling, amazing acting, and a really tight edit. That's what programmers really want, and that's what's ultimately going to entertain, and impress audiences.

Do I need to have this great whiz-bang opening? My film starts kind of slow, and so I feel it's not getting into festivals because of the slow start.

I think if your film is slow to start and hard to get into, it's just hard for programmers to concentrate, especially when they are watching maybe 15 shorts or four features a day. That said, my feeling is the slower the set-up, the bigger the pay-off should be.

When I am watching films, I want to say that my total focus is on the screen, but that is sadly not true. I am often distracted by e-mail, office issues and the phone, I wish I could lock myself in a sealed room, but that is not possible.

Which brings me to ask you about Bloom.

Bloom is one of my favorite success stories. In 2008, I was screening the film *Bloom*, while I was cooking dinner for the screening committee who were on their way to my house. When I first watched it, I was bored out of my mind, because nothing was happening. In the first six minutes of the eight minute film, nothing was happening. Then, all of a sudden, wham — an amazing turn of events and a double-twisted ending! It was incredible. When the committee arrived, I replayed the film and we all agreed — the film was a winner.

Bloom suffered from a problem I see quite often — slow pacing is difficult to program. The film I need to program after such a film needs to be quicker or funnier, and in a climate where few high-quality comedies are being produced, it makes programming a challenge.

After we programmed *Bloom*, I spoke to Lance Larsen [the director], and he mentioned that the film was having problems getting into festivals. I knew what the problem was — the slow beginning. I really loved the film, so I called other programmers and asked them to watch the whole film, slow start and all. They did, and ultimately, the film did very well on the circuit. I am proud that I was able to do a small part in getting the film additional play. The whole scenario points out one of the challenges facing many programmers. Festivals are not perfect, so we try to work with what we have, and change our processes as we can. It is always an ever-evolving process.

Do you ever feel that in your process, some great films get left behind?

Yes, but I have to trust the process I created — which is based on the work by countless other programmers before me. DC Shorts is unique with the feedback component and by having film enthusiasts and not film insiders as the first round of screeners. I have to trust that films which my audience will truly appreciate are the ones with scores and comments that rise to the top. It has been a learning process for me.

A good example is a film we showed in 2011 called *Little Horses*, co-written by Luke Matheny, who had won the Oscar the year before for his short, *God of Love.* It's a nice, slow moving film about a divorced dad trying to win the love of his son. I just thought it was a cute film, but I didn't think it was the best film that season. However, our audiences loved it, and the filmmakers in attendance voted the film as the peer award winner. The film has a quality I think is often missing in many films — heart. You feel for the dad: you feel his pain and you feel his joy. And that's the key.

I was talking to a festival yesterday and they said they're adding a question to their survey for screeners to fill out: *Does this film have heart?* You want a film where the filmmaker is giving their all, but it has heart to connect with an audience. I think that's a great question. I think that's something we're going to be adding to our survey next year.

If my film's not really, really slick, but it does have a lot of heart, am I going to get into festivals?

Probably. Story is king. It always is — and always will be. This an era where everyone has access to great equipment and fantastic editing or SFX software. I have seen a rash of new films all done on iPhones! RED cameras, slick transitions, good sound mixing or design — that is all impressive. But the key is storytelling.

I hate to say this, but I don't think schools are teaching storytelling anymore. Film schools are teaching technique and the sexy parts of filmmaking, but they're not sitting down with students and teaching them how to write a proper story. If you don't have good story, you really have *nothing*. I'd rather show a great story that was shot on a shaky VHS camera than a heartless, soulless film that looks gorgeous.

I'm with you on that. Do I need a trailer? What if my whole film is online? Is that a problem for programming?

I encourage everyone to put a trailer up, though I have to say that most independent trailers are lousy. I don't think filmmakers necessarily understand what trailers are about. Trailers are about selling the emotional connection to a film. If you watch professionally edited trailers in slow motion, you'll see that the audio is rarely synced up to the visual — it's usually a few seconds before or after the scene. Studio trailers are all done in very quick shots — nothing is on screen for more than 36 frames. Most trailers I receive from indie filmmakers are more mini-moviette instead of a modern trailer.

We love to link to trailers on our Festival website. Audiences like to watch, and trailers are easy for the media to get a handle on what the programming in a showcase is about. What I won't link to is an entire film. In fact, if I see that a film is available online to watch, I will either ask the filmmaker to take it down — or I might just pass on the film altogether.

If you're film was available online, it's hard for me to program. Why would someone pay $15 to watch your film when they can watch it for free? So, that's always a potential deal breaker for me.

If you need to put your film online as a screener for festivals, then protect it with a password or use a blind URL. At the end of your festival circuit, when you have exhausted your distribution method, *then* put it online for the world to see.

We started DC Shorts Online this year, and we have over 200 shorts for our audience to watch. All of the content is embedded Vimeo or YouTube files which filmmakers put online themselves. All of the films are from past Festivals, and we will not put this year's content up until about six months after the event.

If I come to your festival, can I sell my DVDs there?

We can't necessarily provide you a table, but if you want to meet people and ask them to buy a DVD, go ahead — more power to you. But while this is cool with me, I think you should ask other festival directors for permission. They might not want you to sell any DVDs until after the film shows. If the audience can buy the disc from you for $10, why would they pay $15 to see the screening?

Do you think film festivals help me to sell my film to distributors?

Some festivals invite or have distributors attached. Many are markets, and that's their purpose. Others, like DC Shorts, have many programmers from other festivals in attendance, who are there to scout material. For years, our catalogs were sent to other festival directors who used it to pick films for their events. We don't get a lot of distributors at our festival because we are at the same time as Toronto, and most are there.

I know other festivals, like LA Comedy Shorts, their entire audience is aimed at the industry. So that's who comes: agents and distributors, because they're looking for people who can create new, funny content. It really depends on the festival. Again, that's part of doing the research. Who's attending — and who's not?

If I don't get my film into Sundance, or SXSW, then what does it really matter about the film festival circuit?

That is really short-sighted thinking. You made a film for people to watch — so get it out there so audiences can watch it! That's really what it's about. You made a film for an audience, so go and find that audience. Your audience might not be the same as Sundance and SXSW. And just because your film plays Sundance or SXSW doesn't necessarily guarantee sold-out audiences watching your film. Their audiences are not any smarter or savvier than audiences elsewhere. They just happen to be at an event that has more buzz around it. I think sometimes the audiences at regional events are much more in tune with the films.

If the festival circuit is your way to get to your film out there, then you have to screen it as much as you can — and get it out to as many audiences as possible. That's all there is to it. I think it's better to play to a small audience of seventy that really gets into the film than waiting for a hypothetical audience of 300+ at an overblown event where audiences are more concerned about being seen than what is being shown.

I'm totally in agreement. But sadly, I hear from filmmakers all the time, "I'm going to get into Sundance, and if I don't, then I guess my film is a failure."

No, your film is *not* a failure — it's just a film that didn't get into Sundance.

Listen, they get 8,000 entries for eighty some slots – do the math. It's almost impossible! Many of the ones that were selected either come with a personal relationship between the filmmaker and programmers, or they were films that were mentored by the Sundance Institute, or they had some sort of producer connection. They were not necessarily all blind submissions, but were films and producers who worked the system to get their film in. It's a different level of play, it's like the major leagues versus little league. I'm not saying that regional festivals are little league — I don't think that at all. I think there are slightly different rules, and to play in the major leagues is often a completely different game.

You've been doing this for quite a while: nine years with DC Shorts and a dozen traveling to film festivals. One of the things I'm hearing from a lot of seasoned filmmakers is that film festivals have changed — it's not the way it used to be. Have film festivals truly changed, or is it just the level of competition is so much more fierce?

Well, first, the competition's much more fierce. As the ability to make a film has become easier, there's just much more content out there. In 2004, we received 78 entries. Last year, we received over 1,200.

Ultimately, I am programming for an audience. I am not programming for myself. It's not The Jon Gann Film Festival — it's the DC Shorts Film Festival. I'm programming for audience members with a particular aesthetic, often at odds with my personal one. As the event becomes more "hip," and my audience skews younger, we need to program more films that attract that audience — and I need to learn what those needs are. I don't necessarily have a problem with that, because you always have to grow with your audience.

I also think that festivals are trying to find films that are telling stories in new ways. Sadly, I believe that some older filmmakers aren't evolving with new storytelling methods. I think that is the greatest advantage for younger filmmakers: they're coming up from a new generation with a new point of view, and a new way of consuming media. This new way to consume media is the biggest challenge in the field, and something I grapple with daily.

What is the worst thing a filmmaker has ever said to you?

Because we open our judging system to filmmakers so they can see the first round screeners' scores and comments, I open myself to a lot of criticism. The few days after rejection letters are emailed, my inbox is full of vitriol and hate. Yes, I get plenty of emails from filmmakers who appreciate the feedback, but there are always a handful — who usually have the lowest scores — who write or call.

I saved my favorite hate voicemail, and use it as a training tool for new screeners. The filmmaker rambles on for a good four minutes about how stupid we were, and that we wouldn't know a good film if it slapped us in the face. I understood his frustration — no one wants to receive a rejection letter. But to address your concern in this manner is no way to gain my respect.

As for nice things, filmmakers are always complimenting the event, and I am happy that they had a great time. The one that sticks in my mind was from a young woman who simply said, "This is the most organized festival I have ever attended." As a perfectionist, this was the greatest compliment I could have received.

What do you see as trends coming forward?

There are so many. First, I wish filmmakers would stop remaking or retreading what is already out there. A good example is vampire stories. This trend was Hollywood's darling for the past few years, but now it is mostly over. Your vampire story is probably not unique, and audiences feel as if they have seen it all. They are fatigued by the genre — after all, it is everywhere — movie theaters, TV, books, internet. Yes, there is a core group that will always like vampire movies, but the majority of audiences are done.

The vampire trend is one, like most, which are calculated, planned and produced by the media empires. They know well ahead of you what themes will be coming to a multiplex near you. After all, they are the ones receiving scripts and requesting spec scripts.

When we run the DC Shorts Screenplay Competition, I see this effect in miniature. About four years ago, we received more than a coincidental share of scripts about soldiers returning from war and adjusting back into civilian life. The next year, we received the completed films based on these screenplays. We showed as many as our audience would tolerate — I can only show so many films of a certain theme before my audience will begin to revolt. Now, this year, we are receiving more and more of these heart-wrenching films, but our audience can only bear to sit through a few of them.

The most troublesome trend I see is really beautiful films with no soul. I mentioned earlier that all of the technical expertise in the world does not make a film with heart — a great script and a solid director who can bring that vision to light does. Start with the writing.

Any final thoughts for filmmakers who are looking into film festivals?

Again, do the research. It's not really that painful. Sit down and spend three full days on creating a list of potential festivals. First, list the ones off the top of your head that you think are the ones you want to play based on the festival's reputation. Then research the ones that are more appropriate for your film's themes, target audience and genre. And finally, email festival directors (off season — not in the middle of their programming time) asking for a catalog or list of previous years' films. Try this...

Dear Jon,

Would you be so kind as to email me a catalog from your last event? I want to see what types of films DC Shorts has shown in the past, so I can determine whether or not your festival is appropriate for my film, Offline, *a short film about one man's hesitation to get out from behind his monitor and into a bar to meet potential mates face-to-face. While the 8-minute parable targets the LGBT community, the message is universal for any person in today's dating pool.*

I've heard such wonderful things about your festival, and before I submit my film, I want to complete my research to make sure that my film is a proper fit for your audience.

Thank you for your time,

If I received that e-mail, I would reply in a heartbeat, because it shows some consideration for both me, and what we're trying to do. I do not care to see a list of other festivals the film has played — I want to discover your film for my audience and not feel that I should be compelled to take it because my colleagues did.

And above all, remember, *"There is a festival for every film, but your film is not for every festival."* I hope this book makes that point very clear.

Made in the USA
Columbia, SC
14 May 2019